Brain-Compatible
Activities for
Mathematics

Grades 2-3

Brain-Compatible
Activities for
Mathematics

Grades 2-3

David A. Sousa

CORWIN

A SAGE Company

For information:

Corwin
A SAGE Company
2455 Teller Road
Thousand Oaks, California 91320
(800) 233-9936
Fax: (800) 417-2466
www.corwinpress.com

SAGE Ltd.
1 Oliver's Yard
55 City Road
London EC1Y 1SP
United Kingdom

SAGE India Pvt. Ltd.
B 1/I 1 Mohan Cooperative Industrial Area
Mathura Road, New Delhi 110 044
India

SAGE Asia-Pacific Pte. Ltd.
33 Pekin Street #02-01
Far East Square
Singapore 048763

Printed in the United States of America.

Library of Congress Cataloging-in-Publication Data

Sousa, David A.
Brain-compatible activities for mathematics, grades 2-3/David A. Sousa.
    p. cm.
Includes bibliographical references and index.
ISBN 978-1-4129-6785-3 (pbk.)
    1. Mathematics—Study and teaching (Primary)—Activity programs. I. Title.

QA135.6.S566 2010
372.7—dc22   2009027817

This book is printed on acid-free paper.

11   12   13   14   15   10   9   8   7   6   5   4   3   2

Managing Editor:	Cathy Hernandez
Executive Editor:	Kathleen Hex
Developmental Writer:	Colleen Kessler
Developmental Editors:	Jeanine Manfro, Christine Hood
Editorial Assistant:	Sarah Bartlett
Production Editor:	Cassandra Margaret Seibel
Copy Editor:	Barbara Corrigan
Typesetter:	C&M Digitals (P) Ltd.
Proofreader:	Wendy Jo Dymond
Cover Designer:	Karine Hovsepian
Illustrators:	Jenny Campbell, Ben Mahan, Mark Mason

Contents

Introduction

Brain-compatible math activities are fun and exciting! These activities are often hands-on and involve partners, group work, and class movement, which many students enjoy. Students frequently say that mathematics is difficult for them. Therefore, as an educator, it is your job to choose materials that are likely to be effective in light of current research on how the brain learns mathematics. This book is filled with activities that are centered on brain research and that are structured to maximize the brain's learning potential.

The activities in this book are designed using a brain-compatible lesson plan format. There are nine components of the plan, but not all nine are necessary for every lesson. Those components that are most relevant to the learning objective should be emphasized:

1. anticipatory set,

2. learning objective,

3. purpose,

4. input,

5. modeling,

6. checking for understanding,

7. guided practice,

8. closure, and

9. independent practice.

Each of the components is described in detail in the book titled *How the Brain Learns Mathematics.* Refer to this book for more brain-compatible math research and other teaching strategies. When using the activities in this book, read through the activity first. Then begin preparations for the lesson. It is best to follow the lesson plan format to ensure maximum learning potential. However, meeting the needs of each student in your classroom is always first and foremost. Be flexible to ensure that all students are learning. Last, have fun! These activities may force you to step out of your comfort zone. Embrace the change, and watch your students' brains at work.

PUT IT INTO PRACTICE

How the brain learns is a fascinating and complex process. Advancements in research and technology are helping us understand specifically how the brain learns math and deals with numbers and mathematical relationships. These remarkable findings are improving teaching and learning dramatically. An educator's understanding and application of instructional approaches that are compatible with what cognitive studies tell us will only aid in his or her classroom success.

Some of the recent research discoveries about the brain can and should affect teaching and learning. For example, research tells us that

- creating and using conceptual subitizing patterns help young students develop the abstract number and arithmetic strategies they will need to master counting;
- just as phonemic awareness is a prerequisite to learning phonics and becoming a successful reader, developing number sense is a prerequisite for succeeding in mathematics;
- information is most likely to be stored if it makes sense and has meaning;
- too often, mathematics instruction focuses on skills, knowledge, and performance but spends little time on reasoning and deep understanding; and
- mathematics can be defined simply as the science of patterns.

A much fuller explanation of these discoveries and their implications for school and the classroom can be found in my book *How the Brain Learns Mathematics*, published by Corwin. This book is designed as a classroom resource to accompany that text. The activities in this book translate the research and strategies for brain-compatible math teaching and learning into practical, successful classroom activities. Some general guidelines provide the framework for these activities:

- Writing is an important component in learning mathematics.
- Studies show that more students are motivated and succeed in classes where teachers use activities that address the various intelligences.
- The use of concrete models for representation of concepts and to help create meaning is beneficial.
- Connecting concepts to the real world creates purpose and meaning. This allows math to seem less abstract.
- Using graphic organizers helps students organize their thinking.
- Solving problems in different ways is beneficial to students.

The activities in this book also are supported by research-based rationale for using particular instructional strategies. These strategies include cooperative learning groups, differentiated instruction, discussion, reflection, movement, manipulatives, visualization, and many others, all of which can increase student motivation and retention of learned concepts.

Scientists continue to explore the inner workings of the brain and will likely continue to discover more and more about learning mathematics. Teachers are challenged to stay current on these new findings, to ensure students are using their brains to the fullest capacity. As we learn more about how the brain learns mathematics, we can develop activities like those seen in this book, which will

- aid in teachers' presenting meaningful instruction to students in the classroom,
- ensure that students are staying focused on and remembering more of what teachers have presented, and
- make teaching and learning more effective and enjoyable experiences.

Teachers should always continue to help students recognize that the learning of mathematics will not only be helpful in their future but will also allow them to understand and appreciate the wonders of the world each day.

Links to Focal Points and Standards

CONNECTIONS TO FOCAL POINTS

This chart shows the National Council of Teachers of Mathematics focal points covered in each chapter.

Grade 2

Focal Points		Page Numbers
Number and Operations: Base-Ten System and Place Value	Develop an understanding of the base-ten numeration system and place value concepts, including comparing and ordering numbers, counting in units, and recognizing place value notation.	2, 4, 7, 11, 14
Number and Operations and Algebra: Addition and Subtraction	Develop an understanding of addition and subtraction facts as well as methods for multidigit computations. Use this understanding to develop quick recall of basic addition facts related to subtraction facts.	24, 27, 31, 35
Measurement	Develop an understanding of the meanings and methods of measuring, including different tools and units. Understand the use of standard units of measure and the inverse relationship between the size of a unit and the number of units used in a particular measurement.	82, 86, 89, 92, 96
Geometry	Develop an understanding of the attributes of two- and three-dimensional shapes, including spatial reasoning and the foundations for area, fractions, and proportions.	112, 114, 118, 122

Grade 3

Focal Points		Page Numbers
Number and Operations and Algebra: Multiplication and Division	Develop an understanding of multiplication and division and basic multiplication facts and division facts. Use properties of addition and multiplication (e.g., commutative, associative, distributive) to apply problem-solving strategies. Relate multiplication and division as inverse operations.	40, 44, 48, 51, 54, 57
Number and Operations: Fractions	Develop an understanding of the meanings and uses of fractions to represent parts of a whole, parts of a set, or points or distances on a number line. Solve problems that involve comparing and ordering fractions using models and common numerators and denominators. Extend understanding of place value to numbers up to 10,000 in various contexts.	62, 65, 70, 73, 77
Measurement	Develop an understanding and proficiency in linear measurement using more precision. Develop skills in measuring with fractional parts of linear units. Form an understanding of perimeter as a measurable attribute, and select appropriate units, strategies, and tools to solve problems involving perimeter.	99, 102, 104, 107
Geometry	Describe, analyze, compare, and classify the attributes and properties of two-dimensional shapes. Combine and transform polygons to make other polygons. Apply attributes and properties of two-dimensional space to solving problems involving congruence and symmetry.	124, 129, 132, 134
Data Analysis	Develop data collection and representation skills. Construct and analyze frequency tables, bar graphs, picture graphs, and line plots and use them to solve problems.	162, 166, 170, 173

CONNECTIONS TO STANDARDS

This chart shows the National Council of Teachers of Mathematics standards covered in each chapter.

Grade 2

Content Standards		Page Numbers
Number and Operations	Understand numbers, ways of representing numbers, relationships among numbers, and number systems.	2, 4, 7, 11, 14
	Understand meanings of operations and how they relate to one another.	24, 27, 31, 35
	Compute fluently and make reasonable estimates.	24, 27, 31

(Continued)

(Continued)

Content Standards		Page Numbers
Algebra	Understand patterns, relations, and functions.	4, 122
	Represent and analyze mathematical situations and structures using algebraic symbols.	35
	Use mathematical models to represent and understand quantitative relationships.	27, 31, 35
	Analyze change in various contexts.	89
Geometry	Analyze characteristics and properties of two- and three-dimensional geometric shapes, and develop mathematical arguments about geometric relationships.	112, 114, 118, 122
	Specify locations and describe spatial relationships using coordinate geometry and other representational systems.	114, 122
	Use visualization, spatial reasoning, and geometric modeling to solve problems.	122
Measurement	Understand measurable attributes of objects and the units, systems, and processes of measurement.	82, 86, 89, 92, 96
	Apply appropriate techniques, tools, and formulas to determine measurements.	82, 86, 89, 92, 96
Data Analysis and Probability	Formulate questions that can be addressed with data, and collect, organize, and display relevant data to answer them.	140, 144, 148, 153, 159
	Develop and evaluate inferences and predictions that are based on data.	140, 144, 148, 153, 159
	Understand and apply basic concepts of probability.	140

Grade 3

Content Standards		Page Numbers
Number and Operations	Understand numbers, ways of representing numbers, relationships among numbers, and number systems.	18, 20, 40, 44, 62, 65, 70, 73, 77
	Understand meanings of operations and how they relate to one another.	40, 44, 48, 51, 54, 57
	Compute fluently and make reasonable estimates.	40, 44, 48, 51, 54, 57
Algebra	Understand patterns, relations, and functions.	40, 44, 48, 77
	Use mathematical models to represent and understand quantitative relationships.	40, 44, 48, 51, 54, 57

Content Standards		Page Numbers
Geometry	Analyze characteristics and properties of two- and three-dimensional geometric shapes, and develop mathematical arguments about geometric relationships.	124, 129, 132, 134
	Use visualization, spatial reasoning, and geometric modeling to solve problems.	104, 124, 129, 132, 134
Measurement	Understand measurable attributes of objects and the units, systems, and processes of measurement.	99, 102, 104, 107
Data Analysis and Probability	Formulate questions that can be addressed with data, and collect, organize, and display relevant data to answer them.	162, 166, 170, 173
	Develop and evaluate inferences and predictions that are based on data.	170, 173

About the Author

 **David A. Sousa**, EdD, is an international consultant in educational neuroscience and the author of seven best-selling books on how to translate brain research into educational practice. For more than 20 years, he has presented at national conventions of educational organizations and has conducted workshops on brain research and science education in hundreds of school districts and at colleges and universities across the United States, Canada, Europe, Asia, Australia, and New Zealand.

Dr. Sousa has a bachelor of science degree in chemistry from Massachusetts State College at Bridgewater, a master of arts in teaching degree in science from Harvard University, and a doctorate from Rutgers University. He has taught high school science, has served as a K–12 director of science, and was superintendent of the New Providence, New Jersey, public schools. He has been an adjunct professor of education at Seton Hall University and a visiting lecturer at Rutgers University. He is a past president of the National Staff Development Council.

Dr. Sousa has also edited science books and published articles in leading educational journals. He has received awards from professional associations and school districts for his commitment and contributions to research, staff development, and science education. He is a member of the Cognitive Neuroscience Society, and he has appeared on the NBC *Today* show and on National Public Radio to discuss his work with schools using brain research.

1

Base-Ten and Place Value

JUMPING JELLYBEANS

Objectives

Students will recognize number patterns in the base-ten numeration system.

Students will use jellybeans to practice counting by tens.

Anticipatory Set

Place a large jar of multicolored jellybeans on your desk or in another widely viewed location. Then invite students to count with you to 100, first by ones and then by twos, fives, and tens. Ask students which method of counting is the slowest (*counting by ones*) and which is the fastest (*counting by tens*).

Purpose

Arithmetic and mathematical knowledge should be based first on concrete situations rather than abstract concepts.

Tell students that they will look for patterns on a hundred board. The patterns that they discover will help them to see how numbers are arranged to show different values. Explain that when you understand the patterns, you can group numbers together to count items faster.

Input

Copy the **Hundred Board reproducible (page 6)** onto an overhead transparency, and give each student a photocopy. Point out how the 10 numerals along the top row are repeated over and over again throughout the board. Guide students to point out various patterns that they find on the board. For example, in the column under *10*, every number ends in *0*. Have students count by tens to 100 again, this time pointing to the numbers on the board as they go along.

Modeling

Show students the jellybean jar. Tell them, "I want to know exactly how many jellybeans are in this jar, but to count them all by myself would take a long time. How might we be able to work together to count these jellybeans?" Allow several students to respond, and then explain that you want them to help you put the jellybeans into groups of 10 so you can count them quickly.

Show students a small paper cup and count aloud as you place 10 jellybeans in the cup. Count out 10 more jellybeans and place them in a separate cup. Say, "There are 10 jellybeans in each cup. I can count by tens, and I know that I have 20 jellybeans so far. You will work in pairs to make sets of jellybeans just like these. Then we can all count by tens together to see how many jellybeans we have in all."

Guided Practice

Organize students into 10 small groups or pairs. Give each group 10 small paper cups and 1 large cup filled with jellybeans. Instruct students to count out 10 jellybeans and place them in 1 cup.

Checking for Understanding

Check to make sure that each group has one cup with 10 jellybeans in it. Ask how many jellybeans should be in each cup (*10*).

Independent Practice

Ask groups to finish counting out the rest of their jellybeans in sets of 10. Circulate and monitor student work and interactions. When all the jellybeans have been counted, ask each group to count by tens to show how many jellybeans they have. Jellybeans that could not be grouped in a set of tens should be counted as ones. Invite a student from each group to use an overhead marker to color the box on the hundred board transparency that matches the number of jellybeans for the group.

Closure

Have groups collect their cups of jellybeans and bring them to a table at the front of the room. Combine all of the single jellybeans into one bowl and have volunteers create sets of 10 with them. Then have students arrange the cups into groups of 10 while counting aloud to 100. Ask, "How many groups of 10 does it take to make 100? How many sets of 100 would it take to make 1,000?" Using the sets of cups as a model, count by hundreds to determine how many jellybeans there are in all. Have students draw pictures in their math journals to show how the jellybeans were grouped and counted.

HUNDRED BOARD-O

Objective

Students will use their knowledge of place value to identify numbers on a hundred board.

Anticipatory Set

Ask students to describe various types of Bingo games that they have played. For example, they may have played Bingo games that used rhyming words, synonyms and antonyms, or addition and subtraction facts. Display a transparency of the **Hundred Board reproducible (page 6)** on the overhead projector. Tell students that they will play a Bingo game using numbers and place value.

> Charts in different arrangements (e.g., 1 to 100) offer many opportunities for students to explore number patterns.

Purpose

Explain to students that each digit in a number has a specific value based on its place within that number. This is called *place value*. The Bingo game that students will play will help them practice identifying numbers by listening to descriptions of place values.

	H	T	O
43		4	3
100	1	0	0
2			2
58		5	8

Input

Draw a place value chart on the board with spaces for hundreds, tens, and ones. Write the numbers *43, 100, 2,* and *58* in a column next to the chart. Fill in the place value chart for the number *43* by writing *4* in the tens column and *3* in the ones column. Explain that the *4* is worth 4 tens, or 40. The *3* is worth 3 ones. Say, "40 + 3 = 43." Ask volunteers to fill in the chart for the remaining numbers.

Modeling

Tell students that as they play this game, you will call out numbers in terms of their place value. Choose a number, such as *56*, and say, "5 tens and 6 ones." Use your overhead transparency of the Hundred Board and cover the square for *56*. Explain that *56* is the same as 5 tens and 6 ones. Point out how the number *5* is in the tens place and the number *6* is in the ones place. Repeat with several more numbers.

Guided Practice

Give each student two copies of the Hundred Board reproducible and several paper squares. Have students cut apart one Hundred Board into separate number squares and place the squares in a paper bag. Organize students into pairs, and explain that each pair will play its own game. Tell students to choose one player to go first. Player 1 draws a number square from his or her bag and describes the number using place value, such as, "3 tens and 1 one." Player 2 then finds the matching number on his or her Hundred Board and covers it with a paper square. Players then switch roles. Tell students that they will continue playing in this manner until one player has an entire row on the board covered horizontally or vertically. That player calls out "BOARD-O!" and wins that round. Players can continue playing rounds until you end the playing period.

Checking for Understanding

Ask if students have any questions. Make sure they understand that they need to describe their numbers based on place value and that they should not name the numbers directly.

Independent Practice

Allow students to play the game with their partners for a designated amount of time. Circulate around the room to make sure students are using place value appropriately. Offer corrective feedback if you notice any errors.

Closure

Encourage students to think about what they learned. Give them 2 minutes to talk with their partners about the activity and reflect on their learning. Suggest that they draw a simple place value chart in their math journals and diagram three numbers using the chart. Then have them complete this sentence frame for each of the three numbers: "The number _____ has _____ hundreds, _____ tens, and _____ ones."

Name _____   Date _____

Hundred Board

1	2	3	4	5	6	7	8	9	10
11	12	13	14	15	16	17	18	19	20
21	22	23	24	25	26	27	28	29	30
31	32	33	34	35	36	37	38	39	40
41	42	43	44	45	46	47	48	49	50
51	52	53	54	55	56	57	58	59	60
61	62	63	64	65	66	67	68	69	70
71	72	73	74	75	76	77	78	79	80
81	82	83	84	85	86	87	88	89	90
91	92	93	94	95	96	97	98	99	100

ORDER UP!

Objective

Students will compare and order whole numbers to 1,000.

Anticipatory Set

Collect a variety of take-out menus from restaurants with which students might be familiar. Staple each menu into a construction-paper folder. Organize students into pairs, and give each pair a restaurant menu and a copy of the **Place Your Order reproducible (page 9).**

Direct students to cut out the two guest checks and take turns acting as a restaurant customer and a server. Tell the server to write down and add up the cost of the customer's order on a guest check. Provide calculators for adding if needed. Afterward, have students hold their guest checks and arrange themselves in order from the least expensive meal to the most expensive. Ask students to read the totals on their guest checks, and help them correct any errors in how they ordered themselves.

Purpose

Tell students that when they worked together with the menu, they used numbers that were less than 100. Explain that in the next activity, they will practice ordering numbers from 0 to 1,000.

Input

Review place value with students. Draw three place value charts on the board with columns for hundreds, tens, and ones. Call on a volunteer to name a number, and write that number in the middle chart. Then ask another student to name a number that is smaller than the first. Write that number in the left-hand chart. Finally, ask a student to name a number that is larger than the first, and write it in the right-hand chart. Ask students to explain how they know which number is largest and which is smallest. Repeat the process with several more numbers.

H	T	O		H	T	O		H	T	O
1	2	2		3	5	6		7	2	9

Modeling

Tell students that they will compare numbers and order them on a giant number line. Hang a clothesline from one end of your room to the other at a height suitable for students to clip numbers to it. Write the numbers *0* and *1,000* on two separate index cards. Use clothespins to clip the *0* at the far-left end of the clothesline and the *1,000* at the far-right end. Gather enough index cards so there are two for each student and two for you. Write one number between 1 and 999 on each index card. Do not duplicate any numbers.

Choose two index cards, and say, "This is the number _____. About where should I place it on the number line?" Invite several students to show you where they think the number belongs. Ask a volunteer to clip it on the clothesline number line. Hold up the second number, and say, "This is the number _____. Is it between 0 and [the first number] or [the first number] and 1,000? About where should I place it on the number line?" Allow several students to show you where they think the number belongs. Ask another volunteer to clip it on the number line.

Guided Practice

Distribute the remaining index cards so each student has two numbers. Have students take turns sharing their numbers and using clothespins to clip them on the number line. Offer corrective feedback when needed.

Checking for Understanding

Make sure students have a good sense of the order of numbers. Ask them about several other numbers, and have them identify which are larger and which are smaller.

> One way to assist students in remembering the meaning of what was learned is to have them write it down in a journal after each lesson where something new is presented.

Independent Practice

Give students a copy of the **Order Up! reproducible (page 10).** Invite them to complete the activity independently. Explain that they will need to write the numbers in correct order on the guest checks.

Closure

Suggest that students answer the following question in their math journals: "What should I look for when I want to put numbers in order from smallest to largest?"

Place Your Order

Guest Check	
1.	
2.	
3.	
4.	
5.	
6.	
Total	

Thank you!

Come again!

Guest Check	
1.	
2.	
3.	
4.	
5.	
6.	
Total	

Thank you!

Come again!

Order Up!

Directions: Look at the numbers in each box. Write them in order from smallest to largest on the blank guest checks.

920	130
65	17
212	

4	1,000
462	62
463	

831	15
108	653
1	

394	823
318	768
444	

10	79
100	85
7	

NUMBER NEIGHBORHOOD

Objective

Students will use randomly drawn digits to create the largest possible number.

Anticipatory Set

Ask students how long it would take them to count to 1,000. Challenge a student to count as high as possible in 2 minutes. Then let a few other students try while you keep track of the time.

Purpose

Tell students that they will play a game today. Their goal is to create the largest number possible. To do this, they will need to remember what they have learned about place value.

Input

Explain to students, "When comparing two numbers, you should look at the far-left digit to judge which number is larger. For example, if you have the numbers *329* and *419*, you would look at the hundreds place and compare *3* and *4*. The number with the *4* in the hundreds place is the larger number. Another way to compare numbers is to look at the number of digits. If one number has four digits and the other has only three digits, the four-digit number is larger."

Modeling

Tell students that they will play a place value game called Number Neighborhood. The object of the game is to make the largest number possible. The player with the largest number in each round gets to move forward on the game board. The person who reaches the last square on the game board first wins the game.

Prepare a game board by gluing the **Number Neighborhood Game Board reproducible (page 13)** to the inside of a file folder. Cut 5 index cards in half to make 10 cards, and then number the cards *0* to *9*. Make a second set of number cards for your opponent, and invite a volunteer to help you demonstrate how to play the game.

1. Each player shuffles a set of number cards and places them facedown in a pile.

2. Each player draws four boxes in a row on a sheet of paper. Players will place cards in these boxes to create four-digit numbers.

3. Each player draws the top card from his or her pile and places it in any of the four boxes. The goal is to create the largest number possible. After players place their cards, the cards cannot be moved.

4. Players continue drawing number cards and placing them in the boxes until all four boxes are filled.

5. Players compare the two 4-digit numbers and decide which number is larger.

6. The player who made the largest number moves his or her game marker forward two spaces on the game board.

7. Players then reshuffle all their cards and play another round. The game continues until one player reaches the end of the path on the game board.

Guided Practice

Let students choose partners to play the game. Give each pair a copy of the Number Neighborhood Game Board reproducible and a file folder. Direct them to glue the page to the inside of the file folder. Then have each student cut five index cards in half and use them to make number cards *0* through *9*. Finally, have them draw a row of four boxes on a sheet of paper and select small objects to use as game markers, such as counters or buttons. Guide students through one round of the game. At the end of the first round, have each pair name the two numbers they created and identify the larger one.

Checking for Understanding

Encourage students to ask questions. Initiate a quick discussion about any strategies that they used in creating the largest possible numbers.

Independent Practice

Allow students to play the game for a designated amount of time. Circulate around the room, and watch for strategies to evolve.

Closure

Bring students back together to discuss the game as a class. Ask questions such as, *What kinds of strategies did you use to play the game?* and *Did they work all the time or just some of the time?* Have students describe at least one strategy they used for the game in their math journals.

Number Neighborhood Game Board

Start

Finish

STRETCHING NUMBERS

Objective

Students will represent numbers in expanded form.

Anticipatory Set

Use a heavy-duty elastic band or other similar item that can be stretched. Attach one end to the classroom doorknob and hold on to the other end. Walk slowly away from the door, pulling and stretching the elastic band as you move. Stretch it as far as you can, acting like you are working very hard. When you cannot stretch the band any farther, stop and say, "Whew! Stretching is hard work!" Make note of where you stopped, and invite a few students to see how far they can stretch the band.

Purpose

Explain to students that numbers can be represented in a variety of ways. One way is called *expanded notation,* which involves writing a number to show the value of each digit. Tell students, "When doing expanded notation, you stretch out the number and turn it into an addition problem." In this activity, students will learn how to write numbers in expanded form.

Input

Ask students to tell you the value of different digits in numbers. Write *432* on the board, and ask, "What is the value of the *3?*" (*30*), "What is the value of the *2?*" (*2*), and "The *4?*" (*400*). Repeat this process for several additional numbers until you are sure students understand the value of digits in numbers.

Modeling

Draw a large grid on the board with four columns and six rows. Label the columns "Thousands," "Hundreds," "Tens," and "Ones." Choose a number with digits in the thousands place and write it in the grid. Write each digit in the correct column according to its value. For example, if your number is *6,539,* write *6* in the Thousands column, *5* in the Hundreds column, *3* in the Tens column, and *9* in the Ones column.

Tell students that you are going to stretch the number into its expanded form as if it were a rubber band: "The *6* in this number has a value of 6,000, so I am going to write *6,000* in the third row." Demonstrate how to write *6,000* in the chart. Then say, "The next digit in the number is *5.* Can anyone tell me the value of the *5?*" (*500*). Write *500* in the fourth row of the chart.

Continue filling in the chart until each digit is represented. Then show students how to write the values in a mathematical sentence to show the original number. Write "6,000 + 500 + 30 + 9" on the board. Read aloud the sentence, and say, "This shows the number *6,539* in expanded form."

Guided Practice

Copy the **Stretch It Out reproducible (page 16)** onto an overhead transparency for each student, and distribute the transparencies with drawing paper, wet-erase markers, and erasers. (Have students place the drawing paper under the transparency. This makes the transparency easier to see.) Then write *7,657* on the board. Guide students through the process of filling out their charts using that number. Continue practicing as a group with a few more numbers, and invite volunteers to write the expanded form of each number on the board.

Thousands	Hundreds	Tens	Ones
6	5	3	9
6			
	5		
		3	
			9

6,000 + 500 + 30 + 9 = 6,539

Checking for Understanding

As you circulate around the room, check students' work to see if anyone still needs more guided practice. Provide students with additional numbers for more practice if needed.

Independent Practice

For in-class practice or homework, give students a copy of the **Stretching Numbers reproducible (page 17)** to complete independently. Explain that they may use the Stretch It Out page to figure out the expanded form of each number, and then they must write each equation on the Stretching Numbers page.

Closure

Have students write a number in expanded form in their math journals and then draw a diagram of the number using base-ten blocks. Direct them to draw cubes for thousands, large squares for hundreds, rectangles for tens, and small squares for ones.

Stretch It Out

Thousands	Hundreds	Tens	Ones

+ _____   + _____   + _____   _____

Name _____ Date _____

Stretching Numbers

Directions: Write the expanded form for each number.

373	

	1,231

422	

	3,789

8,671	

PLACE VALUE PAUSE

Objective

Students will recognize place value to 10,000.

Anticipatory Set

Write the numbers *0* through *9* in black marker on separate sheets of drawing paper, one number per sheet. Make a comma sheet as well. Make the numbers large enough to be seen from far away. Photocopy several sets of numbers and commas to make cards for the activity. If you wish, laminate the sheets for durability. Pass out a number or comma to each student.

Gather students together in a large group. Reinforce number value by giving a variety of directions such as, *Hold up your card if it is the smallest digit, Stand up if you have the largest digit, Raise your hand if your digit has no value,* and *Clap if you can multiply your digit times itself to get* 1.

Purpose

Tell students that they will use the numbers *0* through *9* to practice forming large numbers.

Input

Tell students that a digit's value depends on where it is located in a number. For example, write *56* on the board. Explain that *56* is 5 tens (or 50) and 6 ones. Write the number in expanded form: "$56 = 50 + 6$." Then write "2,957," and ask students the value of *5* in this number (*50*). Then write the number in expanded form: "$2,957 = 2,000 + 900 + 50 + 7$."

Modeling

Tell students that they will be playing a game called Place Value Pause. The object of the game is to work together to form the largest possible number in 10 seconds. When 10 seconds are up, they will pause so their number can be judged by the rest of the class.

Write the numbers *0* through *9* on separate index cards, and place them in a bag. Draw four numbers from the bag, and write them on the board. Call four students with those numbers to the front of the room, along with a "comma" student. Have these students hold their cards in front of them so the class can see the numbers. Ask the class, "Which digit should come first to make the largest number possible?" Guide them to answer the largest digit. Ask them to tell you which digit should come next. Continue until all four digits and the comma are in the correct positions. If needed, position students in the proper order to form the largest possible number. Ask the class to verify the number.

Guided Practice

Explain that five students will now follow the same process without help from the class. Tell students that you will call five of them to the front of the room and that they will have 10 seconds to form the largest possible number. The class will then give them a thumbs-up if the number is the largest possible or a thumbs-down if there is a way to make a larger number.

Call five students to the front of the room (four numbers and one comma), and say, "Go!" Use a stopwatch to time them for 10 seconds, and then shout, "Pause!" Ask the class to verify the number. Play several rounds of the game until students have a good understanding of place value.

Checking for Understanding

To assess understanding of the concept, draw several more sets of numbers from the bag. Invite students to write the largest possible number on a sheet of paper at their desks. Walk around the class, and check student work.

Independent Practice

Leave the number and comma cards in the math center for students to play the game with independently. Invite students to compete in teams, and award points to the team that forms the highest number fastest.

Extend the learning by challenging students to make the smallest numbers possible. You may also decide to add more digits to the numbers, extending into the ten thousands and hundred thousands.

For more practice, place a set of number cards in two bags in the math center. Invite student pairs to play a game to see who can form the larger number. Each student chooses one of the bags and draws numbers from that bag. The student who forms the largest number wins that round.

Closure

Invite students to reflect on the activity in their math journals. Ask them whether forming the numbers with their bodies instead of on paper was a helpful learning technique.

PLACE VALUE BINGO

Objective

Students will understand place value to 10,000.

Anticipatory Set

Gather dried beans, small paper squares, or chips to use as Bingo markers. Copy the **Place Value Bingo Card reproducible (page 22)** onto a transparency, and randomly write the numbers *0* through *9* in the boxes to fill in the card.

As students get ready for math class, sing the "Bingo" song. Encourage students to join in and sing along with you:

There was a farmer, had a dog,

And Bingo was his name-o.

B-I-N-G-O,

B-I-N-G-O,

B-I-N-G-O,

And Bingo was his name-o!

> Keep learning and searching for new ways to have fun with numbers.

Purpose

Explain that the class will use a Bingo game to practice recognizing place value.

Input

Write the number *16,824* on the board. Ask students to identify which digits are in the ones, tens, hundreds, thousands, and ten thousands places, for example, "In which place is the *8?*" (*hundreds*) and "Which number is in the ten thousands place?" (*1*). Write the number in expanded form: "$16,824 = 10,000 + 6,000 + 800 + 20 + 4.$"

Modeling

Give each student a copy of the Place Value Bingo Card reproducible and a handful of game markers. Invite students to write the numbers *0* through *9* randomly in the boxes on their cards. Explain that you will write a number on the board. If students have any digits in the same place column, they should cover them with markers.

Demonstrate using your Place Value Bingo Card transparency. Write a number on the board. (Make sure that the number you write contains at least one digit in the corresponding place on your Bingo card.) For example, if you write the number *93,415*, you might have 3 in the thousands column of your

Bingo card. Cover the *3* with a marker. If you have a *3* in the ones column, you do not cover it.

Guided Practice

After making sure all students have filled in their Bingo cards, write a number on the board. Invite students to mark their Bingo cards if they have one of the digits in the matching column.

Checking for Understanding

Ask if any student marked a digit. Ask him or her to share the digit marked and the column in which it was found. Check to make sure that the digit falls in the correct place column. Repeat several times if needed to make sure students understand how to play the game.

Independent Practice

Continue playing the game by writing new numbers on the board and allowing students to check their Bingo cards and mark any matching spaces. When a student marks five spaces in a row horizontally, vertically, or diagonally, he or she shouts, "Bingo!" Make sure to list the numbers in sequence on the board as you call them so you can go back later and check that the student has all the correct answers. Play as many rounds as time allows.

Closure

Ask students to reflect in their math journals on how playing Bingo helped them learn about place value. Invite them to work with partners to think of other fun games they could play to reinforce this math concept.

Place Value Bingo Card

Ten Thousands	Thousands	Hundreds	Tens	Ones

Multidigit Addition and Subtraction

Sum Roll

Ball Toss

Math Hockey

Fact Family Trees

SUM ROLL

Objective

Students will solve multidigit addition problems.

Anticipatory Set

Before beginning this activity, gather different-colored dice and a set of overhead dice, if possible. Each pair of students will need six dice, three in one color and three in a different color.

Wrap two cube-shaped gift boxes in light-colored paper. Wrap two more boxes in a different-colored paper. Use a marker to draw dots on the cubes so they look like sets of dice. Invite four students to come to the front of the room, and give each student a cube. Have the students all toss their cubes at the same time and report to the class which numbers they rolled. Next, ask each pair of students with matching-colored cubes to add their two numbers. For example, if they rolled a 4 and a 5, they would say, "4 + 5 = 9."

Then ask students to tell which numbers they can make using the two numbers rolled. In this example, the 4 and 5 could make 45 or 54. Continue choosing new groups of four students to take turns rolling the cubes until everyone has had a chance to participate. Then tell students that they will play a game using dice to practice adding numbers.

Purpose

Explain to the students that dice are fun tools for learning different math skills. Today, they will use them to practice math facts and then create and solve multidigit addition problems.

Input

For this demonstration, use overhead dice or two of the box dice. Roll the dice, and add the numbers aloud. Roll again, and call on a student to add the numbers. For several minutes, continue rolling the dice and asking students to find the sums. Explain that this is an easy way to practice math facts.

Modeling

Tell students that they will use their knowledge of simple math facts and apply it to solving problems with larger numbers. Show them two dice of one color and two dice of another color. Roll the first set of dice, and discuss the results: "I rolled my green dice and got a 5 and a 3. I will write those two numbers on my record sheet."

Place a transparency of the **Sum Roll Record Sheet reproducible (page 26)** on the overhead projector, and show students how to write each number on one of the die shapes next to box 1. Then say, "I will put these two numbers together to make 35. Which other two-digit number could I make with these numbers?" (53) "Yes, 53. I could write either 35 or 53 in box 1. I think I will use 53." Write 53 in the top of box 1 on the reproducible.

Continue, saying, "Now I will roll the other two dice. I got a *9* and a *1*. I will write those two numbers on the next two die shapes on the reproducible. Which two numbers can I make using a *9* and *1?*" (*91 and 19*). "Yes, *91* and *19*. I will use *91* and write it in box 1 under *53*. Now I have an addition problem to solve."

Review the steps for solving addition problems with two digits, including regrouping. Write the answer to your equation (*144*) under the problem. Then also write the answer in box A on the right side of the page. Explain that the answer to each problem must also be written in the box on the right so all the sums can be totaled at the end of the game. The player with the largest total wins the game.

Guided Practice

Divide the class into student pairs. Give each pair two copies of the Sum Roll Record Sheet reproducible, along with six dice (three of one color for one student and three of a different color for the other student). Tell students that they will take turns using two dice to create three addition equations using two-digit numbers. After that, they will roll three dice to create three equations using three-digit numbers. Once partners have created and solved all six equations, they can use a calculator to add the six sums and write the answer in the Total box. The player with the highest sum wins the game.

Walk through the steps to help students form their first equation. Remind students to write each individual number rolled in the die shapes. Then they may decide which two-digit number they want to form using the single-digit numbers. Give students time to play the game while you circulate around the room and check students' equations.

Checking for Understanding

Monitor students while they play the game. Midway through the game, have students take a break so you can model rolling six dice to form an equation using three-digit numbers. Solve as a class, and ask if there are any questions that need clarification. Then allow students to finish their game.

Independent Practice

Place several sets of colored dice and copies of the Sum Roll Record Sheet in the math center. Encourage students to visit the center individually. Challenge them to a contest to see which student can achieve the highest total sum in the class. Help students create a graph to show the results of the contest.

Closure

Roll your overhead dice to create two 3-digit numbers. Write the numbers on the board in the form of an addition equation. Invite students to solve the equation in their math journals. Then have them write in their journals about their experiences playing this game. Offer writing prompts such as the following: *How can this game help you learn and practice math facts? Did you use a strategy while playing this game? What was your strategy? Did it help you?* and *Why do you think it did or did not work?*

Sum Roll Record Sheet

Directions: Roll the dice. Write the numbers in the die shapes. Use the numbers to make addition problems. Solve the problems. Copy the sums in the boxes, and then use a calculator to add up the total.

1. [+ _____]

2. [+ _____]

3. [+ _____]

4. [+ _____]

5. [+ _____]

6. [+ _____]

A.

B.

C.

D.

E.

F.

TOTAL

BALL TOSS

Objective

Students will practice solving multidigit subtraction problems.

Anticipatory Set

Before beginning this activity, create a ball-toss box. Get a large box (copy paper boxes work well), and use cardboard pieces and strong tape to divide the inside of the box into 10 equal-sized sections. Label each section with one digit, from *0* to *9*. Find two small, soft balls that will fit into the sections to use for the game. Place the box at the front of the classroom or other open area, and tape a line on the floor several feet from the box.

To begin the math lesson, randomly toss one ball to different students and have them toss the ball back to you. Invite students to practice their throwing and catching skills.

Purpose

Explain to students that they will play a ball-tossing game while practicing their subtraction skills. After reviewing basic subtraction facts, they will create two-digit numbers to form subtraction problems.

0	1
2	3
4	5
6	7
8	9

Input

Display the ball-toss box that you made. Tell students that they will warm up for the game by practicing simple subtraction facts. Ask students to line up single file behind the line on the floor. Then ask a student to stand next to the box so he or she can call out the numbers. Stand at the front of the line and toss each ball, one at a time, into the box. Aloud, subtract the smaller number from the larger number.

Tell students, "For this relay race, you will toss the balls into the box and subtract the two numbers aloud. Then you run to the box, get the balls, and hand them to the next student in line. That student then takes a turn. Once you take your turn, sit down on the floor. Make sure to say your equation and the answer loud enough for everyone to hear. Let's see how fast we can get through the line. I will stand by the box and tell you your numbers." Time the game, and record the results on the board.

Modeling

After the relay, tell students that in the next game, they will use the box and balls to make two-digit subtraction problems. Ask for two volunteers to help you demonstrate. Place a transparency of the **Toss an Equation reproducible (page 29)** on the overhead projector. Show students how to create problems using this procedure: Ask the first student to toss the balls in the box, one at a time. Write the numbers in the first two balls of the problem. Have the next student repeat the process while you write those numbers on the remaining two balls.

With the class, examine the four numbers, and use them to form two new two-digit numbers. Write the larger number in the top two boxes and the smaller number in the bottom two boxes. Review the steps for subtraction with and without regrouping. Have students help you solve the equation. Repeat this process several times, calling on new volunteers for each new equation.

Guided Practice

Give each student a copy of the Toss an Equation reproducible. Have two students at a time toss the balls into the box and write their numbers on the board. Let the students who tossed the balls determine which numbers to form for the equation. Have all students copy the equation onto their reproducibles and solve the problem. Solve the equations on your transparency, but turn the overhead projector off so students cannot see the answers. Continue play until the reproducible is filled or time is up.

Checking for Understanding

Turn on the overhead projector, and ask students to check their work against yours. Tell them to use a colored pencil or pen to correct any mistakes. Remind students that checking their work helps them to see whether they need more practice.

Independent Practice

Invite students to work independently or with a partner to solve the equations on the **Toss It! Practice reproducible (page 30).** They can complete the reproducible in class or as homework.

Closure

Invite students to respond to the following questions in their math journals: "Why are games like Ball Toss a good way to practice math facts? What did you like about the game? What didn't you like about the game?"

Toss an Equation

Directions: Write the numbers from the Ball Toss game in the circles. Form two-digit numbers to create subtraction problems. Then solve.

1. ○ ○
   ○ ○ − [ ][ ]
              [ ][ ]

2. ○ ○
   ○ ○ − [ ][ ]
              [ ][ ]

3. ○ ○
   ○ ○ − [ ][ ]
              [ ][ ]

4. ○ ○
   ○ ○ − [ ][ ]
              [ ][ ]

5. ○ ○
   ○ ○ − [ ][ ]
              [ ][ ]

6. ○ ○
   ○ ○ − [ ][ ]
              [ ][ ]

7. ○ ○
   ○ ○ − [ ][ ]
              [ ][ ]

8. ○ ○
   ○ ○ − [ ][ ]
              [ ][ ]

9. ○ ○
   ○ ○ − [ ][ ]
              [ ][ ]

10. ○ ○
    ○ ○ − [ ][ ]
               [ ][ ]

Toss It! Practice

Directions: Solve the problems below.

1.   56
    − 45
    ‾‾‾‾

2.   69
    − 12
    ‾‾‾‾

3.   91
    − 56
    ‾‾‾‾

4.   84
    − 32
    ‾‾‾‾

5.   67
    − 14
    ‾‾‾‾

6.   93
    − 30
    ‾‾‾‾

7.   97
    − 22
    ‾‾‾‾

8.   83
    − 18
    ‾‾‾‾

9.   72
    − 13
    ‾‾‾‾

10. 60
    − 11
    ‾‾‾‾

MATH HOCKEY

Objective

Students will estimate sums and differences.

Anticipatory Set

On the floor, use tape to create a playing field by dividing a large square into four equal boxes. Label the top two boxes "A" and "B," and label the bottom two boxes and "B" and "A." Tape a starting line several feet away from the playing field. Photocopy and cut out the cards from the **Math Hockey Game Cards reproducible (page 33).** Place each set of cards in separate paper bags labeled "A," "B," and "C," and set them aside.

Bring in a toy hockey stick and a toy hockey puck. Or you could use a broom for a hockey stick and an empty, clean tuna can wrapped in masking tape for a puck. If possible, wear a hockey jersey to class on the day you plan to do this activity. Put on a hockey mask, wave your stick while holding the puck, and shout, "Let's play!"

Purpose

Tell the class that they will play a game called Math Hockey to practice estimating sums and differences. Explain that estimating can help them when they need to know an approximate number or amount.

> Keep learning and searching for new ways to have fun with numbers.

Input

Write the problems "28 + 34," "45 – 9," "63 + 27," and "37 – 18" on the board. Ask students to estimate the sums and differences. Tell them that since *28* is almost *30* and *34* is close to *30*, you can add *30* and *30* to get an estimate of *60*. Repeat this process for the remaining three problems.

Modeling

Explain to students that they will use the hockey equipment to determine the numbers for which they will estimate sums and differences. Display the A, B, and C bags. Draw a C card to find out which operation to use—addition or subtraction.

Then grab your hockey gear, place your puck at the start line, and gently use the stick to slide the puck toward the playing field. Choose a card from the A or B bag, depending on the space in which your puck lands. Repeat and draw a second card. Write the numbers on the board with the operation symbol in between them. Estimate the solution to the problem. For example, say, "I drew a plus sign and the numbers *514* and *120*. *514* is close to *500*, and *120* is close to *100*. 500 + 100 = 600. I estimate the sum to be *600*."

Guided Practice

Give every student in the class a chance to play the hockey game using the stick and puck. While they are playing, have students record the numbers, equations, and solutions on a piece of scrap paper. You can record the equations as well, using a transparency.

Checking for Understanding

Display the transparency so students can check their work. If they made mistakes, ask them to write in the correct answers using a different-colored pencil or pen. If you like, have students find the actual answers to each equation and compare them to the estimates. Answer any questions they have, and clarify any misunderstandings.

Independent Practice

Invite students to work in pairs to complete the **Math Hockey Practice reproducible (page 34).** Have them work together to solve the problems and check their answers.

Closure

Tell students that they will have 2 minutes to reflect on what they learned about estimating sums and differences. Then they will share their thoughts with a partner. Afterward, have them write in their math journals about the benefits of estimating in real life. Prompt students with questions such as, *When might you need to estimate if you are eating out? Shopping?* and *Can you think of other situations in which estimating might be useful?* If students need help thinking of ideas, suggest things such as preparing food for a party, planning the amount of time needed to complete different activities, determining the distances between two places, and so on.

Math Hockey Game Cards

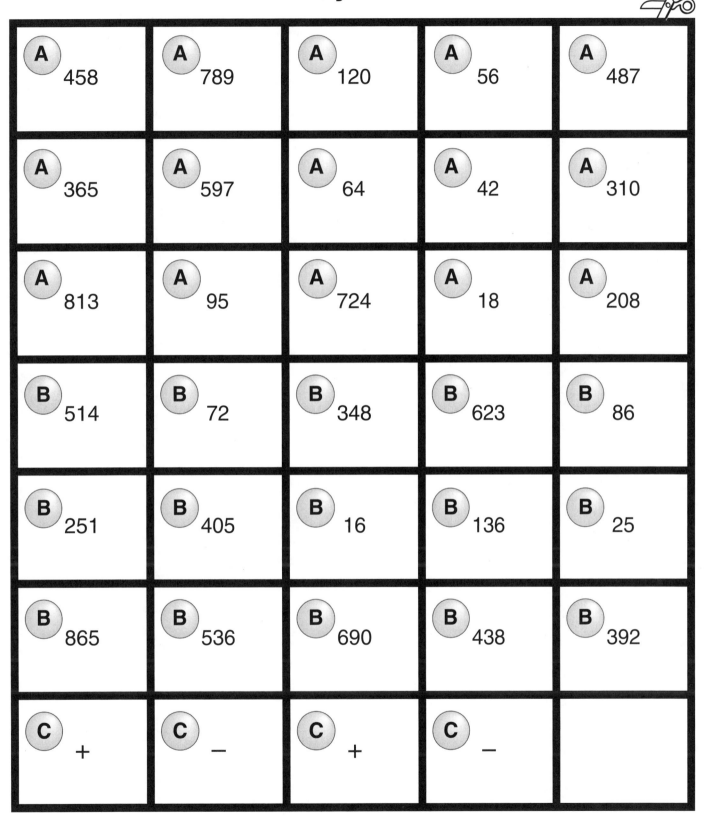

A 458	A 789	A 120	A 56	A 487
A 365	A 597	A 64	A 42	A 310
A 813	A 95	A 724	A 18	A 208
B 514	B 72	B 348	B 623	B 86
B 251	B 405	B 16	B 136	B 25
B 865	B 536	B 690	B 438	B 392
C +	C −	C +	C −	

Math Hockey Practice

Directions: Estimate the sums and differences. Check your answers with a partner.

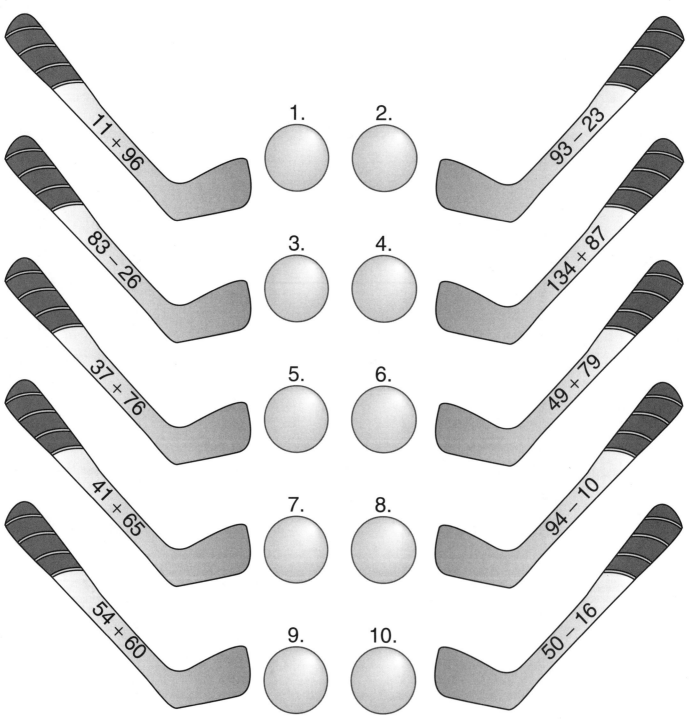

11 + 96

93 − 23

1.

2.

83 − 26

134 + 87

3.

4.

37 + 76

49 + 79

5.

6.

41 + 65

94 − 10

7.

8.

54 + 60

50 − 16

9.

10.

FACT FAMILY TREES

Objective

Students will use random numbers to form fact families and discuss the relationship between the equations.

Anticipatory Set

Draw a diagram of a simple family tree on the chalkboard. Write your name and the names of your parents in the diagram. Explain to students that a family tree shows the relationships between the members of a family. Encourage students to draw their own simple family trees. Continue to explain that groups of numbers can also be related to one another. Tell students that *fact families* are groups of numbers that are related to each other and can be used to make a set of math equations.

Purpose

Tell students that in this lesson, they will work with numbers to create fact families. The numbers that make up the fact families will be used to create two addition equations and two subtraction equations.

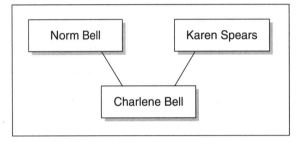

Input

Explain that numbers in equations can be rearranged to form related equations. These numbers are called *fact families*. Write the numbers *3, 4,* and *7* on the board. Show students that these numbers can be arranged into four related equations. While writing the problems on the board, say, "I can write $3 + 4 = 7$, $4 + 3 = 7$, $7 - 3 = 4$, and $7 - 4 = 3$. All problems use the same three numbers and are related to one another. This is a fact family for the numbers *3, 4,* and *7.*"

Ask students to offer equations to form a fact family for the numbers *6, 2,* and *8.* Complete other single-digit fact families as necessary to facilitate student understanding before moving into the activity.

Modeling

Copy the **Fact Family Trees reproducible (page 37)** onto an overhead transparency, and place it on the overhead projector. Tell students that they will use polyhedron dice to generate numbers to use for their fact families. Demonstrate rolling two polyhedron dice. Say, "I rolled a *12* and a *7.* To make a fact family, I will use these numbers to create a third number. I can add them or subtract them to get the third number." Show students how to add the numbers ($12 + 7 = 19$) and how to subtract the numbers ($12 - 7 = 5$).

Explain that each equation results in a different fact family. One fact family has the numbers *19, 12,* and *7,* while the other fact family has the numbers *12, 7,* and *5.* Tell students you will choose the fact family for *12, 7,* and *5.* Write the numbers on a tree shape on the reproducible. Point out how the largest of the three numbers should be written at the top of the tree. Then ask for student volunteers to produce two addition equations and two subtraction equations for the fact family ($7 + 5 = 12$, $5 + 7 = 12$, $12 - 7 = 5$, $12 - 5 = 7$). Write the equations on the tree trunk.

Guided Practice

Invite students to help you find three more fact families to complete the Fact Family Trees reproducible on the overhead. Pass the dice around the room, and have students roll them to find the numbers for each fact family. Have volunteers write the numbers for the fact families on the tops of the trees and the equations on the tree trunks.

Checking for Understanding

Give each student a copy of the Fact Family Trees reproducible. Roll the dice again, and tell students which numbers you rolled. Have students work in pairs to determine a third number (based on the first two numbers) that can be used to create a fact family. Have partners work together to complete one fact family tree using the three numbers. Ask the pairs to present their fact families to the class and show the equations that they listed. If students make mistakes, help them to correct their work.

Independent Practice

Give each student a pair of polyhedron dice. Invite students to work independently to complete the three remaining fact family trees on their reproducibles.

Fact Family Trees

Closure

Tell students that they have 2 minutes to share their fact families with a partner. Then have them answer the following question in their math journals: "How does working with fact families help you to better understand addition and subtraction?"

Fact Family Trees

Directions: Roll your dice. Use the numbers to create a fact family. Write the numbers for the fact family in the top of the tree. Write the equations for the fact family on the tree trunk.

3

Multiplication and Division

TRAY ARRAYS

Objective

Students will use arrays to demonstrate multiplication facts.

Anticipatory Set

Make a transparency of the **Cookie Tray reproducible (page 42)** to use for the activity. If desired, bring in cookies (or other small treats) to share with the class at the end of the lesson.

Read to the class the book *Amanda Bean's Amazing Dream* by Marilyn Burns. Point out the different arrangements of items in the pictures. Focus special attention on the pastries on the trays. Explain that the items are arranged in a certain configuration called an *array*. An array is made up of objects arranged in rows and columns.

Purpose

Tell students that they will practice working with meaningful models, arranged in arrays, to solve multiplication problems.

Input

Give students 5 minutes to say their times tables to a partner. Assign each pair a number group, such as the *2s*, *3s*, or *5s*. When time is up, ask students which number group is the most difficult to remember. Most students have the most difficulty with the number groups *7* and *8*.

Modeling

Place a transparency of the Cookie Tray reproducible on the overhead projector. With an overhead marker, draw 12 cookies arranged in a 2×6 grid. Write the equation shown with the array: "$2 \times 6 = 12$." Explain that there are two rows of 6 cookies, which equals 12 cookies.

Erase the 12 cookies, and then draw 20 cookies arranged in a 4×5 grid. Ask students to tell you the equation for that array. Write the answer on the transparency: "$4 \times 5 = 20$." Work several more examples on the overhead, asking volunteers to provide the equations for the arrays shown.

Guided Practice

Give each pair of students several small manipulatives to represent cookies. Have each student take turns with his or her partner in forming arrays. Call out a multiplication problem, such as $3 \times 9 = 27$, and have one student form the array. Tell his or her partner to check the array and give a thumbs-up if the array is correct. Ask partners to help each other fix the array if it is incorrect.

Ask partners to switch roles. Then call out, "6 × 4 = 24," and have students repeat the process. Continue the activity using several additional problems. Circulate around the room and monitor student work.

Checking for Understanding

Observe students carefully as you walk around the room. If you notice that a student is making several mistakes, offer immediate corrective feedback.

Independent Practice

Give each student a copy of the **Tray Arrays reproducible (page 43).** Allow students to work independently or with partners to complete the reproducible.

Closure

Pass out cookies (or other treats) to students. Instead of cookies, you might give students cut-up vegetables and fruit. Form a simple array on each student's desk. After each student has identified the array, invite him or her to enjoy the snack. During snack time, ask students to draw and identify several arrays in their math journals.

Cookie Tray

Tray Arrays

Directions: Look at each array. Then write the multiplication problem for the array.

1.
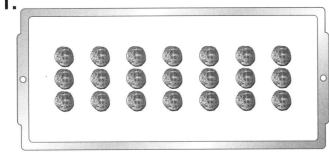
_____

2.
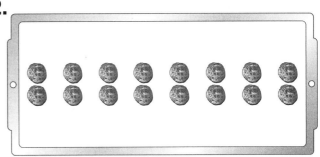
_____

3.
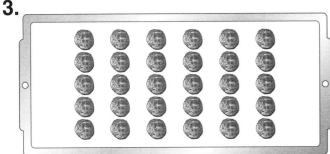
_____

4.
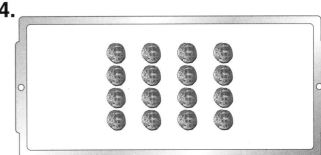
_____

Directions: Draw a cookie array to show each multiplication problem.

5. $4 \times 9 = 36$

6. $3 \times 8 = 24$

GRAPE GROUPS

Objective

Students will use grapes to represent division using equal groups.

Anticipatory Set

Before this activity, gather several bunches of grapes. Separate the bunches so that each bunch can be evenly divided. Make an enlarged copy of the **Bunch of Grapes reproducible (page 46)** to use for the activity. Cut out each grape in the bunch, secure it to the board with tape, and then draw a stem and a vine.

To begin the lesson, tell students the familiar Aesop's fable *The Fox and the Grapes*. If possible, find an illustrated version to read aloud to students. Ask students questions about the story, such as, *Why did the fox want the grapes so badly? How many grapes are in a bunch? Do you like grapes?* and *Are grapes sour, like the fox said, or sweet and juicy?*

Purpose

Tell students that they will be practicing division using equal groups of grapes. They will learn that using equal groups is a method they can use to find quotients until they have memorized their division facts.

Input

Have students solve some simple division problems, such as those with *2* as the divisor. Then give them a few more challenging problems to try. Tell students, "Some division problems are easier to solve than others. Using models can help you solve problems while you practice. Today we will be using grapes as models."

Modeling

Tell students that you will begin by using the large bunch of grapes that you taped to the board. Explain that there are 24 grapes. Write "$24 \div 2 = 12$" on the board. Tell students that most people can divide by 2 in their heads, but you're going to show them what this problem looks like when you model it as equal groups. First, have students count the grapes with you as you point.

Then tell students, "This problem tells me that we are going to divide these 24 grapes into two equal groups." To separate the grapes into two equal groups, place one grape to the left and one grape to the right. Ask students to count along with you as you regroup the grapes, one by one. When the grapes are divided into two equal groups, ask students to count and tell you how many grapes are in each group (*12*). Explain that this model shows the problem $24 \div 2 = 12$.

Place all the grapes back in the middle of the board in one bunch, and repeat the process using the problem $24 \div 3 = 8$.

> Recognizing the number of objects in a small collection is part of innate number sense.

Invite volunteers to come to the board to separate the grapes as the rest of the class counts aloud. Depending on the level of your students, continue working with the grapes for the following problems: $24 \div 12 = 2$, $24 \div 8 = 3$, $24 \div 6 = 4$, and $24 \div 4 = 6$.

Guided Practice

Give 18 grapes to each student pair. (You can use actual grapes or any manipulatives that you call *grapes* for this lesson.) Ask pairs to divide their grapes into equal groups and then write the corresponding equations. Encourage students to explore all of the possibilities. They should eventually come up with four equations: $18 \div 2 = 9$, $18 \div 9 = 2$, $18 \div 3 = 6$, and $18 \div 6 = 3$. Walk around the room while students explore their grape groups, and offer guidance as necessary.

Checking for Understanding

Ask students if they have any questions about how to separate the grapes into equal groups. Provide assistance as needed.

Independent Practice

Give students a copy of the **Grape Groups reproducible (page 47)** to complete independently. Explain that they will need to look at the starting number in the bunch of grapes, draw grapes to show equal groups, and then record the division problem on the line. This allows them to apply what they learned using models in a more abstract way.

Closure

Invite students to parade around the room singing, "I heard it through the grapevine! Division was easy to do this time! Eighteen divided by 2 is 9! Division was easy to do this time! Yummy, yummy, yeah!" Call out additional problems, and have students shout out the answers as they sing and march. Ask students to draw an example of dividing a larger group into smaller equal groups in their math journals. Have them record the matching division problem.

Bunch of Grapes

Grape Groups

Directions: Count the number of grapes in each bunch. Write the number on the line. Then divide that number of grapes into equal groups. Draw the groups. Write the equation on the line.

1. How many grapes? _____  Divide the grapes into 3 equal groups. Equation: _____	2. How many grapes? _____  Divide the grapes into 4 equal groups. Equation: _____
3. How many grapes? _____  Divide the grapes into 2 equal groups. Equation: _____	4. How many grapes? _____  Divide the grapes into 5 equal groups. Equation: _____

BUTTON FACT FAMILIES

Objective

Students will use buttons to model multiplication and division fact families.

Anticipatory Set

Gather buttons, chips, or other small circular manipulatives. If you are unable to find small, button-shaped manipulatives, use a large, circular hole punch to create your own by punching circles out of paper or cardstock.

Ask students, "Have you ever played the button game? It's simple! Whoever is 'It' hides the button, and everyone else tries to find it. 'It' gives 'hot' and 'cold' clues. For example, if someone is close to the button, 'It' might tell that student, 'You are getting warmer!'" Play a game with students. Show them a small button. Tell them to close their eyes while you walk around the room and hide the button. Stop at several different places before and after the one where you decide to hide the button. Then ask students to open their eyes and find the button. As students search, offer clues such as, *Trevor is getting warmer. . . . Oh, Allie is ice cold!* When someone finds the button, that student will be "It" the next time you play the game.

Purpose

Explain that you will use buttons to form arrays that model multiplication and division fact families.

Input

Ask students to list equations in the addition and subtraction fact families for the numbers *2*, *3*, and *5* (*2 + 3 = 5, 3 + 2 = 5, 5 − 2 = 3, 5 − 3 = 2*). Encourage them to recall several additional fact families for addition and subtraction.

Tell students that multiplication and division have fact families as well. For example, the fact family for the numbers *3*, *5*, and *15* is *3 × 5 = 15, 5 × 3 = 15, 15 ÷ 3 = 5*, and *15 ÷ 5 = 3*. Explain that just like with addition and subtraction, they can use fact families to help see relationships between numbers and their equations.

Modeling

Tell students that they will be building arrays out of buttons to show multiplication and division fact families. Remind them that arrays can be used to model multiplication and division facts. Draw a button array on the board with four rows of five buttons each. Explain that this array can show four facts.

Say to students, "Four rows times 5 buttons in each row equals 20 buttons, or 4 × 5 = 20. I can also read it this way: five columns times 4 buttons in each column equals 20 buttons, or 5 × 4 = 20. If I were reading it to show division,

I could say 20 buttons divided by four rows equals 5 buttons in each row, or $20 \div 4 = 5$. Or I could say 20 buttons divided into five columns equals 4 buttons in each column, or $20 \div 5 = 4$." Explain that this shows all four equations in the *4, 5,* and *20* fact family.

Guided Practice

Draw a 3×6 button array on the board. Call on individual students to talk about the different problems represented by the array. Have each student identify one of the equations and write it on the board next to the array. Once all of the equations are listed, write "Fact Family for *3, 6,* and *18*" on the board above the equations.

Repeat this process for several other fact families, drawing the arrays and asking different students to offer an equation that can be made using the array you've drawn.

Checking for Understanding

Ask students to draw an array on pieces of paper. You could either tell them which dimensions to use or have them choose. Then tell them to write the equations and label the fact family. Circulate around the room, and look over students' papers as they work. If you notice that many students are still having trouble, work out several more fact families on the board. Otherwise, offer additional help to just those who are struggling with the concept.

Independent Practice

Have students work individually or in pairs to complete the **Button Fact Families reproducible (page 50).** Remind them to label the name of the fact family after they finish writing the four equations represented by the array.

Closure

In their math journals, have students reflect on how models can help them identify fact families.

Button Fact Families

Directions: Look at each button array. On the lines next to the array, write the equations in the fact family. Then write the fact family at the top.

Fact Family: _____

_____

_____

_____

_____

Fact Family: _____

_____   _____

_____   _____

Fact Family: _____

_____   _____

_____   _____

Fact Family: _____

_____   _____

_____   _____

Fact Family: _____

_____

_____

_____

Fact Family: _____

_____

_____

_____

OPPOSITES ATTRACT

Objective

Students will understand that multiplication and division are inverse operations.

Anticipatory Set

Place two large horseshoe magnets on the overhead projector. (The shadows of the magnets will show on the screen.) Placing the same poles next to each other, use one magnet to push the other around the overhead. Then flip one magnet and show how the opposite poles attract.

Purpose

Tell students, "Opposite, or inverse, operations in math connect like the opposite poles of a magnet. You can use this connection to help you check your work when solving math problems."

Input

Ask students to explain the relationship between addition and subtraction. Guide the discussion until students make the connection that addition and subtraction are opposite operations. Explain that they can add two numbers and then subtract one of the addends from the sum to get the other addend. Demonstrate this for students as a refresher. Write "$7 + 8 = 15$" and "$15 - 8 = 7$" on the board. Explain that this is a way to check the answer. Tell students, "Since subtraction is the opposite of addition, when you subtract the addend *8* from the sum *15* and get the other addend, *7*, you know that your answer is correct." Explain that this is the same for multiplication and division. They are opposite operations. Students can use one to check the other.

Modeling

Demonstrate this concept for students by writing "$5 \times 8 =$" on the board. Ask students to raise their hands and tell you the answer to this equation. Write it on the board: $5 \times 8 = 40$. Tell students that they can check to see if this answer is correct by dividing their answer by one of the numbers in the equation. Then write "$40 \div 8 = 5$" and "$40 \div 5 = 8$." Explain that the multiplication problem was correct because you know that $40 \div 8 = 5$ and $40 \div 5 = 8$.

Guided Practice

Write several additional multiplication problems on the board. Walk through two or three with students. Then use the answer and one of the numbers in the problem to create a division problem to check your work. Have students solve additional problems with partners while you circulate and assess their understanding.

Checking for Understanding

Write the problem "12 × 3 =" on the board. Have students solve the multiplication problem on a sheet of paper. Then tell them to write a division problem next to it to check their answers. Walk around the room quickly, looking at each student's paper. If you notice that many students did not arrive at the correct answer, walk the class through another problem on the board.

Independent Practice

Give students copies of the **Opposites Attract reproducible (page 50).** Have them work independently to solve the problems. Explain that they need to solve the multiplication problem that is on the positive pole of the magnet and write a division problem to check their work on the negative pole. Work through the sample problem with students before they get started.

Closure

Have students turn to partners and explain why knowing that multiplication and division are inverse operations can be helpful in studying math. Then invite them to reflect on what they learned in their math journals.

Opposites Attract

Directions: Solve the multiplication problem. Then write a division problem to check your answer. The first one is done for you.

1. 12 × 2 = [24] [24] ÷ [12] = [2]

2. 5 × 6 = [ ] [ ] ÷ [ ] = [ ]

3. 11 × 8 = [ ] 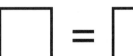 [ ] ÷ [ ] = [ ]

4. 9 × 3 = [ ] [ ] ÷ [ ] = [ ]

5. 8 × 4 = [ ] [ ] ÷ [ ] = [ ]

6. 7 × 10 = [ ] [ ] ÷ [ ] = [ ]

7. 12 × 8 = [ ] [ ] ÷ [ ] = [ ]

8. 7 × 6 = [ ] [ ] ÷ [ ] = [ ]

9. 5 × 11 = [ ] [ ] ÷ [ ] = [ ]

10. 10 × 3 = [ ]   [ ] ÷ [ ] = [ ]

SHOW ME THE MONEY!

Objective

Students will estimate and multiply multidigit numbers by single-digit numbers.

Anticipatory Set

Copy the **Show Me the Money! Record Sheet reproducible (page 56)** onto a transparency for the lesson. Then gather a variety of catalogs and newspaper advertisements.

To begin the lesson, sit at your desk and pore over a catalog. Mumble phrases to yourself, such as, "How much would two of these cost? Hmmm . . . three, carry the two . . . no, no . . . four, carry the six, times two. . . . Oh, I just can't do it!" Look up and ask students if they can help you figure out how much two items priced at $79.65 would cost. Allow them some thinking time and then say, "Wait a minute! I have an easier way!"

Purpose

Tell students that they will be using newspaper advertisements and catalogs to practice multiplying large numbers mentally.

Input

Ask if students recall how to estimate. Explain that estimating is making your best guess about the value of something. So when you are trying to figure out the value of two items priced at $79.65, you can estimate that each item costs $80.00. The problem 80×2 is much easier to manage than 79.65×2.

Modeling

Explain that in this activity, students will work with partners to spend $1,000. They will decide on an item that they want to purchase, decide on a quantity, and figure out about how much it will cost (or estimate the cost). Their goal is to come as close to $1,000 as possible. Tell them that they must purchase two or more of every item they choose so that they can practice multiplying in their heads.

Write "$129.95" on the board. Tell students that you want to purchase three televisions that cost $129.95 each. Display the Show Me the Money! Record Sheet on the overhead. Write "television" in the Item column. Ask students to tell you the estimated price for this item (*$130*). Write this estimate in the Estimated Price column. In the Quantity column, write *3*. Then ask students to multiply 130×3. Write the product, *$390*, in the Total column.

Guided Practice

Hand a student a catalog, and ask him or her to choose an item and a quantity. Write the price of the student's chosen item on the board, and ask a volunteer to give you the item's estimated price. Write this number on the Record Sheet. With students' help, continue filling in the Record Sheet for this item and the quantity the student chose. Ask how much more money they must spend to get to $1,000.

Independent Practice

Group students into pairs, and distribute a Show Me the Money! Record Sheet and a pile of ads and catalogs to each pair. Tell them to work together to spend $1,000. Remind them that they must buy at least two of each item they are interested in so that they can practice mental multiplication.

Closure

Have students discuss with their partners the benefits of estimation when they are dealing with large numbers. Then have them list in their math journals all the ways that estimating can benefit them in their daily lives (e.g., figuring out a tip for a meal).

Show Me the Money! Record Sheet

Directions: Look through catalogs and ads to find things to buy. Record your purchases on the chart below.

Item	Estimated Price	Quantity	Total

DRAW AND DIVIDE

Objective

Students will model division problems by forming groups.

Anticipatory Set

Display a large pad of chart paper on an easel. When students are gathered for the lesson, tell them that the class is going to play a drawing game. Explain that you will draw a picture on the chart paper and they will raise their hands to guess what you are drawing.

Draw 12 apples arranged in three groups of four. After students guess a few times, explain that you have drawn a division equation. You represented the equation $12 \div 3 = 4$ using 12 apples in three groups of four.

Purpose

Tell students that drawing pictures to represent division problems is a strategy that can make problem solving easier for them. In this activity, students will be using pictures to model division problems.

Input

Ask students to tell you the answers to some common division problems. This will allow them a few minutes to warm up and practice their math facts. Call out several problems, such as, "25 divided by 5! 18 divided by 9!" Continue in this manner for several minutes. Explain that all of these division problems can also be modeled using objects or pictures separated into equal groups.

Modeling

Tell students that you will draw another division problem on the chart paper. Draw 28 stars separated into four groups of 7. Write the division equation underneath the picture: "$28 \div 4 = 7$." Ask students to say the problem with you: "28 stars divided into four groups equals 7 stars in each group." Repeat this process with one or two more problems before moving on to Guided Practice.

Guided Practice

Give each student a copy of the **Draw and Divide reproducible (page 59).** Ask for a student volunteer to come to the chart paper and draw a picture for the first problem on the page: 32 stars divided into eight groups. Ask him or her to write the division equation underneath the picture ($32 \div 8 = 4$). Tell the students to do the same on their own papers so they can compare their answers with your volunteer's answer. Talk the class through this problem as you did previously: "32 stars divided into eight groups equals 4 stars in each group."

Checking for Understanding

Ask students if they understand how to proceed with the reproducible. Invite them to give you a thumbs-up or thumbs-down. If many students are showing a thumbs-down, provide another group example on the chart paper. If only a few students indicate that they are still confused, assist them individually as they continue to work on their reproducibles.

Independent Practice

> Practice may not make perfect, but it does make permanent, thereby aiding in learning retention.

Have students complete the reproducible. You may choose to have students complete these problems in small groups using chart paper so they can compare and discuss answers. Or you may invite them to work individually.

Closure

Gather the class together at the chart paper, and ask for another volunteer to draw a division problem. Give that student a problem to draw by whispering it in his or her ear. Encourage the rest of the class to guess the problem. Repeat this as many times as needed to assess learning. Or you may choose to play a team game. The first player to guess the matching equation for the picture earns one point for his or her team. After several rounds, the team with the most points wins!

Give each student a slip of paper with a division problem written on it. Ask students to draw a picture representing their problems in their math journals.

Draw and Divide

Directions: Draw the groups shown. Write the division problem beneath your picture.

1. 32 stars divided into 8 groups. Equation: _____	2. 40 diamonds divided into 5 groups. Equation: _____
3. 49 hearts divided into 7 groups. Equation: _____	4. 27 balls divided into 9 groups. Equation: _____
5. 12 oranges divided into 4 groups. Equation: _____	6. 16 triangles divided into 2 groups. Equation: _____
7. 54 buttons divided into 9 groups. Equation: _____	8. 22 pencils divided into 2 groups. Equation: _____

4

Fractions

FRUITY FRACTIONS

Objective

Students will compare fractional amounts.

Anticipatory Set

Gather several pieces of fruit (apples, oranges, and bananas work well), a cutting board, and a knife. Write the fractions $\frac{1}{2}$, $\frac{1}{3}$, and $\frac{1}{6}$ on the board. Ask students to vote for the fraction they think is the largest by writing it on a slip of paper.

Purpose

Tell students that they will be using fruits to compare fractional amounts.

Input

With students counting aloud, tally their votes on the board. Draw tally marks under the appropriate fractions as you count. Write the total votes, and circle the number under each fraction when you finish. Ask for student volunteers to explain why they voted as they did. Ask them to share what they already know about fractions with a partner.

Modeling

Take three pieces of the same type of fruit, along with the cutting board and knife, to the front of the room. Cut one piece into halves. Set one-half on the table. Cut the next piece of fruit into thirds, and set one-third next to the first piece on the table. Finally, cut the last piece of fruit into sixths, and set one-sixth next to the other two pieces.

Ask students to share their observations. Explain that when numerators are the same, a larger denominator is actually a smaller fraction.

Guided Practice

Write $\frac{3}{4}$, $\frac{3}{5}$, and $\frac{3}{7}$ on the board. Ask students to tell you which fraction is largest ($\frac{3}{4}$). Then have students work with a partner to put the fractions in order from largest to smallest ($\frac{3}{4}$, $\frac{3}{5}$, $\frac{3}{7}$). Have them write their answers on individual whiteboards or pieces of scrap paper. Then give students a copy of the **Fruity Fractions reproducible (page 64).**

Checking for Understanding

Check students' work by having them hold up their whiteboards or papers. If you notice that many students are having trouble ordering the fractions correctly, give them three more fractions to order, making sure the numerators are the same.

Independent Practice

Have students work in pairs or independently to practice ordering fractions and complete the reproducible.

Closure

Bring students back together. Write three fractions on the board, and ask them which is the largest. Repeat the fruit-cutting activity by inviting individual students to demonstrate different fractions for the class. Include different fruits to show a variety of sizes and shapes. When you're finished, invite students to eat the fruit while they reflect on the activity in their math journals.

Name _____ **Date** _____

Fruity Fractions

Directions: Write the fractions in order from smallest to largest. Remember, the smaller the denominator, the larger the fraction.

Example: $\dfrac{2}{6}$  $\dfrac{2}{4}$  $\dfrac{2}{3}$

1. $\dfrac{1}{8}$, $\dfrac{1}{4}$, $\dfrac{1}{9}$ _____, _____, _____

2. $\dfrac{2}{3}$, $\dfrac{2}{9}$, $\dfrac{2}{5}$ _____, _____, _____

3. $\dfrac{9}{23}$, $\dfrac{9}{32}$, $\dfrac{9}{12}$ _____, _____, _____

4. $\dfrac{5}{6}$, $\dfrac{5}{7}$, $\dfrac{5}{8}$ _____, _____, _____

5. $\dfrac{4}{9}$, $\dfrac{4}{15}$, $\dfrac{4}{6}$ _____, _____, _____

6. $\dfrac{3}{47}$, $\dfrac{3}{15}$, $\dfrac{3}{8}$ _____, _____, _____

7. $\dfrac{1}{79}$, $\dfrac{1}{85}$, $\dfrac{1}{74}$ _____, _____, _____

8. $\dfrac{8}{9}$, $\dfrac{8}{13}$, $\dfrac{8}{12}$ _____, _____, _____

9. $\dfrac{6}{60}$, $\dfrac{6}{50}$, $\dfrac{6}{30}$ _____, _____, _____

10. $\dfrac{4}{8}$, $\dfrac{4}{6}$, $\dfrac{4}{7}$ _____, _____, _____

PIECES OF PIZZA

Objective

Students will use pizza manipulatives to represent equivalent fractions.

Anticipatory Set

Give students copies of the **Fraction Pizzas** and **Equivalent Fractions Record Sheet reproducibles (pages 67–69).** Make transparencies of these pages as well, and color the pizzas with permanent markers. Each of the four overhead pizzas should be a different color. Cut them into different fractional sections. For example, color the first pizza blue, and cut it into halves. Color the second pizza green, and cut it into thirds. Color the next pizza yellow, and cut it into fourths. Finally, color the last pizza red, and cut it into twelfths.

Brandish a chef's hat, and shout, "Pizza time!" Toss a pizza made out of cardboard into the air and catch it to capture students' attention. Ask students to tell you their favorite pizza toppings. Then prompt students to start thinking about fractions by asking questions such as, *How many pieces of pizza do you like to eat?* and *What fraction of a pizza is that?*

Purpose

Explain that students will use pieces of pizza to compare fractions. They will then find equivalent fractions.

> Attaching a positive emotion to the mathematics lesson not only gets attention but also helps students see mathematics as having real-life applications.

Input

Ask students what the word *equivalent* means. Explain that the word *equal* has the same meaning—one thing has the same value as another. In mathematics, some fractions are equivalent, but they look different and have a different name. Demonstrate with an example by drawing a circle on the board and separating it into six equal sections. Shade in three sections and ask, "If you ate three pieces of this pizza, what fraction of the pizza did you eat?" ($\frac{1}{2}$ or $\frac{3}{6}$). Write both fractions under the circle. Point out that these fractions are equivalent.

Modeling

Place the pizza transparency that is cut into halves on the overhead projector. Place the halves next to each other so a whole pizza is displayed. Tell students that this is one whole pizza. Split the pizza into two pieces. With an overhead marker, write " $\frac{1}{2}$ " under each piece.

Then ask students how many fourths it takes to make one half (*two*). Place two of the pizza fourths over one of the half pieces to demonstrate that they are the same size. Write " $\frac{1}{2} = \frac{2}{4}$ " under these pieces.

Guided Practice

Distribute the Fraction Pizzas and Equivalent Fractions Record Sheet reproducibles, and have students color and cut out the pizza pieces. Ask students if they can make another equivalent fraction for ½ using one of the remaining pizza pieces. Give them a minute to explore the 3-slice and the 12-slice pizzas. Walk around the classroom, and assess student understanding. When you notice that the majority of students have come to the conclusion that they cannot make an equivalent fraction with the three-slice pizza, but $\frac{6}{12}$ is equivalent, demonstrate this concept using your transparency pizza pieces.

Independent Practice

Gather students into groups of two or three. Have them work together to find as many equivalent fractions as they can with their four pizzas. Ask them to write each set of equivalent fractions on their Equivalent Fractions Record Sheets.

Closure

Ask students to illustrate and list several equivalent fractions in their math journals. They can use these lists later to study for math tests. The illustrations will help them visualize and remember these equivalencies.

Fraction Pizzas

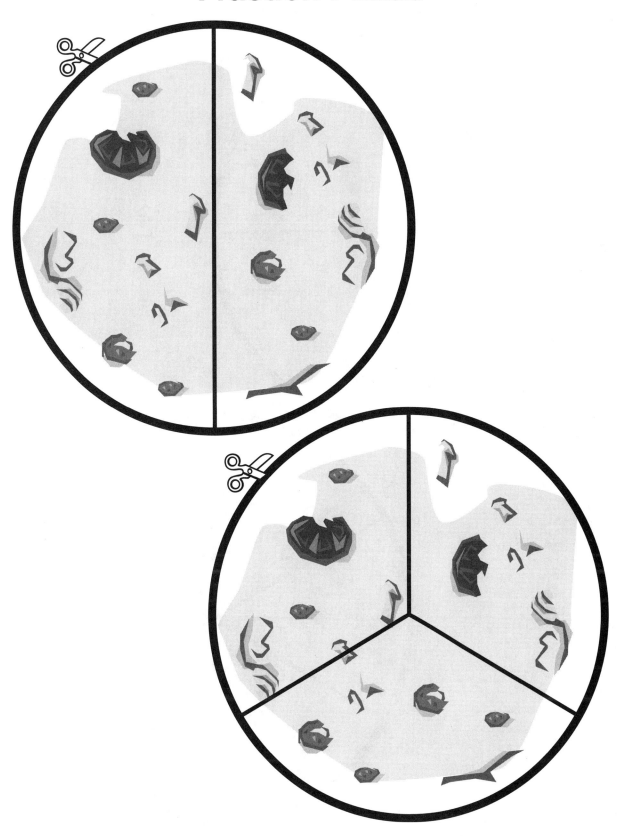

Fraction Pizzas

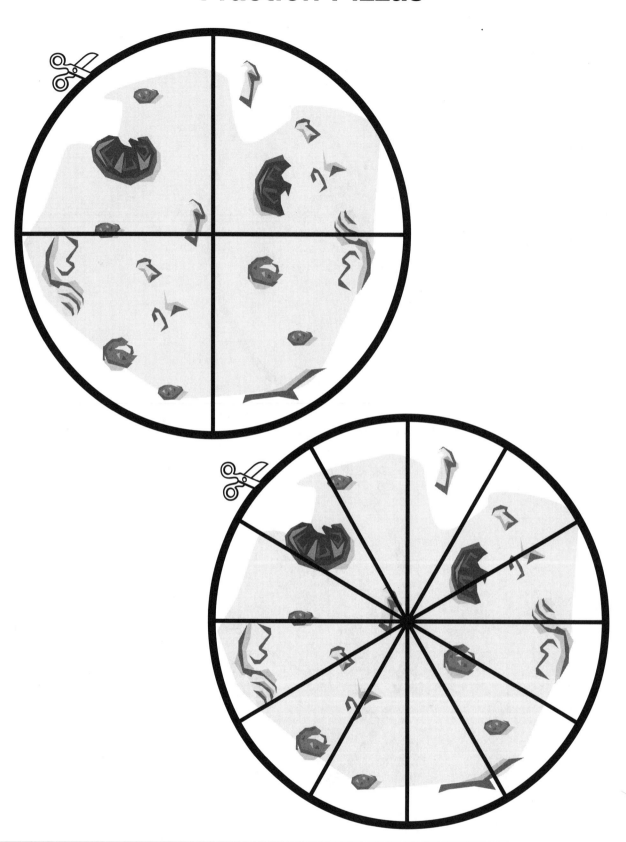

Equivalent Fractions Record Sheet

Directions: Use your fraction pizzas to find the equivalent fractions. Write the equivalent fractions on the lines below.

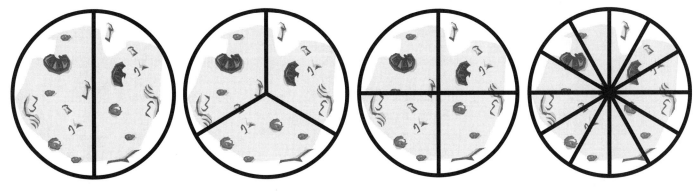

1. $\dfrac{1}{4}$ = _____

2. $\dfrac{1}{3}$ = _____

3. $\dfrac{2}{4}$ = _____ = _____

4. $\dfrac{2}{3}$ = _____

5. $\dfrac{3}{4}$ = _____

6. $\dfrac{4}{4}$ = _____ = _____ = _____

TREASURE HUNT

Objective

Students will understand that fractional amounts are relative to the size of the whole.

Anticipatory Set

Before beginning this lesson, hide a "treasure" on the seat of your desk chair. You might want to hide larger treats (like homework passes) for the winning team and smaller treats (like fun pencils, pens, and stickers) for the winners to pass out to classmates.

Draw a large *X* on the board. When students ask what it is for, tell them, "Usually, *X* marks the spot. But actually, we're going to play a game in which *clues* mark the spot!"

Purpose

Tell students that they will be using their knowledge of fractions to solve a clue that will lead them to a treasure.

Input

Ask if students can identify the following fraction: two out of a group of eight. Praise students when they respond with $2/8$. Then challenge them to come up with another fraction for the same amount. If they are able to tell you $1/4$, praise them again, and explain that these are equivalent fractions. They have the same value and can be used interchangeably.

Modeling

Write on the board, "First $4/5$ of *treat* + first $1/2$ of *suds* + last $2/4$ of *cure*." Explain that the clues to this treasure hunt will take this form. Students will need to look carefully at each word to determine which letters represent the corresponding fractional amount.

Tell students, "In this clue, the first $4/5$ of *treat* is *t-r-e-a*. The first $1/2$ of *suds* is *s-u*. The last $2/4$ (which is equal to $1/2$), of *cure* is *r-e*. If you put those letters together in order, you have *t-r-e-a-s-u-r-e*, which spells the word *treasure*. At the end of the hunt, if you solved the clues to each word correctly, you will have directions to find the treasure."

Guided Practice

Give students a copy of the **Treasure Hunt Clues reproducible (page 72).** Direct students as follows: "Look at the first clue on your Treasure Hunt Clues sheet. Number 1 reads, 'Last $1/3$ of *any* + first $2/3$ of *out*.' Which letter or letters fit the first part of the clue?" (*y*). "Which letter or letters fit the second part of the clue?" (*ou*). "Which word can you spell when you put those letters together?" (*you*). Explain that they will be following this process for all of the clues on the reproducible.

Checking for Understanding

Ask if there are any questions before you allow students to begin solving the rest of the clues. Have them give you a thumbs-up (yes) or thumbs-down (no) to indicate whether they understand.

Independent Practice

Gather students into mixed-ability groups of two or three. Have them work together to solve the clues on the reproducible. Circulate around the room, and offer assistance as needed, reminding students that some of the fractional amounts may refer to equivalent fractions. Celebrate as a class when students find the treasure.

Closure

Write on the board, "Last ⅔ of *who* + last ½ of *door* + last ²⁄₄ of *play.*" Ask students to solve this puzzle in their math journals (*hooray*). Congratulate them on a lesson well done, and distribute the treats.

Treasure Hunt Clues

Directions: Solve each clue to find the letters to form each word. All the words will form a statement that tells you where to find the treasure!

1. Last $\frac{1}{3}$ of **any** + first $\frac{2}{3}$ of **out** = _____

2. First $\frac{2}{3}$ of **cat** + last $\frac{1}{3}$ of **tan** = _____

3. First $\frac{1}{2}$ of **finish** + first $\frac{1}{7}$ of **drought** = _____

4. Last $\frac{1}{4}$ of **many** + last $\frac{3}{6}$ of **devour** = _____

5. First $\frac{1}{3}$ of **higher** + last $\frac{2}{3}$ of **add** + first $\frac{1}{4}$ **endanger** = _____

6. First $\frac{3}{4}$ of **tree** + first $\frac{2}{6}$ of **asking** + last $\frac{3}{7}$ of **measure** = _____

7. First $\frac{2}{4}$ of **what** + last $\frac{3}{5}$ of **there** = _____

8. Last $\frac{1}{5}$ of **chant** + first $\frac{2}{4}$ of **heat** = _____

9. First $\frac{2}{7}$ of **terrify** + first $\frac{3}{4}$ of **ache** + last $\frac{1}{4}$ of **remember** = _____

10. First $\frac{1}{4}$ of **shoe** + first $\frac{1}{3}$ of **ice** + last $\frac{2}{6}$ of **fights** = _____

TAKE A BIGGER BITE!

Objective

Students will compare and order fractions.

Anticipatory Set

On the board, draw the profile of a shark with a large open mouth facing left. Draw another profile of an open-mouthed shark facing right. Invite students to tell you what they know about sharks. Guide students toward the fact that sharks are usually hungry and like to eat a lot. Explain that in this activity, hungry sharks will be eating fractions.

Purpose

Tell students that they will be using hungry sharks to help them remember how to show which fractions are larger. Explain that when comparing fractions, they use the greater than and less than signs. Draw a greater than and a less than sign on the board next to the corresponding shark. Point out how each sign resembles one shark's open mouth.

> Human memory recall often works by association; that is, one thought triggers another in long-term memory.

Input

Ask students to recall how to tell if one fraction is bigger or smaller than another. Remind them that they should look at both the numerator and the denominator. The only time they should compare the numerators is when the denominators are the same. Explain that they most likely can't compare the numerators of fractions that have different denominators.

Modeling

Write $\frac{1}{6}$ and $\frac{4}{6}$ on the board. Ask students to identify which of the fractions is larger. Tell students, "Because the denominators are the same, all we have to do is look at the numerators. The fraction with the greater numerator is larger. I am going to write $\frac{4}{6}$ next to the shark's mouth showing the greater than sign." Remind students that a good way to remember which sign to use is to pretend it is an open mouth that wants to eat the larger number. That way, they always draw the open end toward the larger number.

Continue, explaining that sometimes they will have two fractions with different denominators. They will need to make the denominators the same before comparing the fractions. Write $\frac{3}{4}$ and $\frac{7}{12}$ on the board. Say, "The denominators are different, so even though it looks like $\frac{7}{12}$ is bigger, we need to make the denominators the same to be sure." Explain that when they change the denominator of a fraction, they need to change the numerator as well. To make the denominators the same, you must find a common factor. In these fractions, the common factor is *12*.

They must then multiply the denominator in ³/₄ by 3: 3 × 4 = 12. However, to keep the fractional amount equivalent, they must multiply the numerator by 3 as well. Whatever they do to the denominator, they must also do to the numerator: 3 × 3 = 9. The new fraction is ⁹/₁₂. The fraction ⁹/₁₂ is bigger than ⁷/₁₂, so the shark's open mouth (greater than) should be pointing toward that fraction.

Guided Practice

Remind students how important it is to make sure the denominators are the same before comparing fractions. Write ⁵/₈ and ⁹/₁₆ on the board. Ask students to work with partners to compare these two fractions. Walk around, and see that they are all on task. When it seems that most students have finished, discuss the answer, and make sure that everyone changed the fraction ⁵/₈ to ¹⁰/₁₆.

Checking for Understanding

If you notice that some students are having difficulty making equivalent fractions, gather them into a small group, and work through several more problems before allowing them to work independently.

Independent Practice

Give students copies of the **Take a Bigger Bite! reproducibles (pages 75–76).** Making equivalent fractions can be difficult for some students. They may need practice comparing fractions with the same denominators first. Decide which group your students fall into. Are they able to compare fractions without difficulty? Do they need to work on comparing fractions with the same denominators before they compare those with different denominators?

Based on their ability levels, you may choose to give all students the same Take a Bigger Bite! reproducible or start them off with activity 1 and progress to activity 2. Activity 1 focuses on comparing fractions with the same denominators; activity 2 moves to the next level, focusing on changing denominators and then comparing fractions.

Closure

Have students answer the following question in their math journals: "Why is it important to make sure the denominators are the same before comparing fractions?"

Name _____   Date _____

Take a Bigger Bite! Activity 1

Directions: Compare each pair of fractions. Write < or > in the circle.

Remember!

If the first fraction is larger, use the "greater than" sign. >

If the first fraction is smaller, use the "less than" sign.   <

---

1. $\dfrac{2}{3}$ ◯ $\dfrac{3}{3}$

2. $\dfrac{7}{8}$ ◯ $\dfrac{2}{8}$

3. $\dfrac{9}{12}$ ◯ $\dfrac{6}{12}$

4. $\dfrac{1}{4}$ ◯ $\dfrac{3}{4}$

5. $\dfrac{6}{9}$ ◯ $\dfrac{3}{9}$

6. $\dfrac{12}{12}$ ◯ $\dfrac{5}{12}$

7. $\dfrac{8}{4}$ ◯ $\dfrac{4}{4}$

8. $\dfrac{9}{10}$ ◯ $\dfrac{8}{10}$

9. $\dfrac{3}{5}$ ◯ $\dfrac{4}{5}$

10. $\dfrac{2}{9}$ ◯ $\dfrac{1}{9}$

11. $\dfrac{2}{6}$ ◯ $\dfrac{12}{6}$

12. $\dfrac{17}{10}$ ◯ $\dfrac{11}{10}$

13. $\dfrac{4}{3}$ ◯ $\dfrac{6}{3}$

14. $\dfrac{8}{7}$ ◯ $\dfrac{7}{7}$

15. $\dfrac{5}{5}$ ◯ $\dfrac{9}{5}$

16. $\dfrac{8}{12}$ ◯ $\dfrac{10}{12}$

$\dfrac{1}{12}$ $\dfrac{16}{12}$

$\dfrac{9}{12}$

$\dfrac{8}{12}$

Take a Bigger Bite! Activity 2

Directions: Compare each pair of fractions. Write <, >, or = in the circle.

Remember!

If the first fraction is larger, use the "greater than" sign. >

If the first fraction is smaller, use the "less than" sign.   <

If the fractions are equivalent, use the "equal" sign.   =

Before comparing fractions, make sure the denominators are the same.

---

1. $\dfrac{2}{3}$ ◯ $\dfrac{3}{4}$ ◯ ___ ___

2. $\dfrac{3}{8}$ ◯ $\dfrac{1}{4}$ ◯ ___ ___

3. $\dfrac{5}{10}$ ◯ $\dfrac{1}{2}$ ◯ ___ ___

4. $\dfrac{1}{3}$ ◯ $\dfrac{3}{8}$ ◯ ___ ___

5. $\dfrac{4}{6}$ ◯ $\dfrac{2}{3}$ ◯ ___ ___

6. $\dfrac{1}{2}$ ◯ $\dfrac{4}{7}$ ◯ ___ ___

7. $\dfrac{3}{8}$ ◯ $\dfrac{5}{16}$ ◯ ___ ___

8. $\dfrac{2}{4}$ ◯ $\dfrac{5}{7}$ ◯ ___ ___

9. $\dfrac{5}{6}$ ◯ $\dfrac{5}{8}$ ◯ ___ ___

10. $\dfrac{2}{5}$ ◯ $\dfrac{3}{4}$ ◯ ___ ___

11. $\dfrac{9}{12}$ ◯ $\dfrac{6}{4}$ ◯ ___ ___

12. $\dfrac{8}{3}$ ◯ $\dfrac{10}{9}$ ◯ ___ ___

$\dfrac{1}{2}$ $\dfrac{1}{4}$

$\dfrac{9}{12}$

$\dfrac{8}{12}$

FRACTION COOKIE BARS

Objective

Students will calculate fractions to double a recipe.

Anticipatory Set

Don a chef's hat, and place a mixing bowl, mixing spoon, and several measuring cups and measuring spoons in front of you on a table. Pretend to read a recipe from a cookbook, or use the **Fraction Cookie Bars Recipe reproducible (page 79).** Tell students you are going to make a recipe, but you need to double it to serve the whole class. Read aloud some common fractional amounts of ingredients, such as $\frac{1}{2}$ *cup of sugar,* $2\frac{1}{4}$ *cups of flour,* and $\frac{3}{4}$ *teaspoon of salt.* Pretend you are confused, and ask students, "How can I figure out how to double these fractions? What if I wanted to make only one-half of this recipe? How would I figure out how much of each ingredient to use?" Accept all reasonable answers.

Point out the importance of fractions in cooking. Then ask students to share other ways people use fractions in their everyday lives. In addition to students' responses, mention examples such as shopping, measuring, weighing, calculating, and estimating. Explain that many people use fractions in their jobs, such as engineers, scientists, construction workers, tailors, accountants, and many more.

Purpose

Tell students that they will be calculating fractions using a cookie bar recipe.

Input

Discuss how to double fractions. Write several simple fractions on the board, such as $\frac{1}{2}$, $\frac{1}{4}$, and $\frac{1}{3}$. Using illustrations as a visual reference, demonstrate shading in two halves of a shape ($\frac{1}{2} + \frac{1}{2}$), which equal 1, or the whole. Continue by shading in $\frac{2}{4}$ of a shape ($\frac{1}{4} + \frac{1}{4}$) and $\frac{2}{3}$ of a shape ($\frac{1}{3} + \frac{1}{3}$). Write each equation underneath the corresponding illustration. Suggest that you can also multiply each fraction by 2.

Modeling

Write the following sample ingredients on the board: "$2\frac{3}{4}$ cups flour, 1 teaspoon baking soda, $\frac{1}{2}$ teaspoon baking powder, and $\frac{1}{4}$ teaspoon salt." Explain that you need to double these ingredients. Ask students, "What can I do to double these ingredients? I can add them together, or I can multiply them by 2." Say, "I need $2\frac{3}{4}$ cups of flour. If I double that, I get $4\frac{6}{4}$ or $5\frac{2}{4}$ or $5\frac{1}{2}$." Repeat this procedure for each of the ingredients, asking student volunteers to help with the conversions.

Guided Practice

Give students a copy of the Fraction Cookie Bars Recipe reproducible. Ask students to imagine that there is going to be a school bake sale, and they will need to double this recipe to have enough cookie bars for the sale. Work with students to double the first ingredient, 1 cup softened butter. Ask a volunteer to explain the two methods they can use for doubling (*adding the numbers together and multiplying by 2*). Show students how to write the conversion: "2 cups softened butter." Work through the first three ingredients with students, and then have them work independently or with partners to complete the entire recipe.

Checking for Understanding

Before students begin to work independently, make sure they understand how to proceed. Make sure they understand that they are doubling the recipe, which means each ingredient needs to be doubled for the recipe to work.

Independent Practice

Have students work through the recipe, doubling each ingredient and recording it on the reproducible. If you wish, encourage more advanced students to triple, quadruple, or halve the recipe for larger or smaller results.

Closure

If time and resources allow, work as a class to actually make the fraction cookie bars. Double or triple the recipe, depending on the size of your class. Allow students to help you with the conversions so they receive hands-on, real-life experience with converting fractions. When the cookies are cooled, ask students to help you figure out how to cut up the bars (and name corresponding fractions) so that everyone receives an equal amount. Before cooking anything in class, make sure to check with parents for any food allergies or diet restrictions.

Ask students to respond to the following question in their math journals: "How might doubling fractions help you in other areas besides cooking?"

Name _____ Date _____

Fraction Cookie Bars Recipe

Directions: Double the ingredients for this recipe. Write the measurements in the chart.

Fraction Cookie Bars

Single Recipe	**Double Recipe**
1 cup softened butter	_____ softened butter
2 cups sugar	_____ sugar
4 eggs	_____ eggs
2 tsp. vanilla	_____ vanilla
$1\frac{1}{3}$ cups flour	_____ flour
$\frac{3}{4}$ cup unsweetened cocoa	_____ unsweetened cocoa
1 tsp. baking powder	_____ baking powder
$\frac{1}{2}$ tsp. salt	_____ salt
$\frac{2}{3}$ cup chopped nuts (omit in the event of allergies)	_____ chopped nuts (omit in the event of allergies)

- -

$\frac{1}{3}$ cup butter	_____ butter
6 ounces softened cream cheese	_____ softened cream cheese
$\frac{1}{3}$ cup sugar	_____ sugar
2 Tbs. flour	_____ flour
2 eggs	_____ eggs
$\frac{3}{4}$ tsp. vanilla	_____ vanilla

Cream together wet ingredients listed above the dotted line.
In separate bowl, mix together the dry ingredients listed above the dotted line.
Gradually add dry ingredients to wet ingredients, and then add nuts.

Follow the same steps for the ingredients listed below the dotted line.
Spread half of the first mixture into a greased baking pan.
Spread second mixture over chocolate mixture.
Then spread the rest of the first mixture over the top.
Swirl the batter with a spatula or fork.
Bake at 350 degrees Fahrenheit for 40 minutes or until cookie bars
pull away from side of baking pan. Cool in pan. Then cut into bars or squares.

Makes about 2 dozen cookies.

5

Measurement

MEASURING TOOLS

Objectives

Students will experiment with a variety of measuring tools.

Students will choose appropriate tools to conduct specific measurements.

Anticipatory Set

Place several measuring tools, such as teaspoons, measuring cups, rulers, and scales, on a table at the front of the room. Show students a bag of rice, and tell them you need to measure the amount. Encourage students to offer different solutions for measuring the rice, and then decide as a class which method to use. Ask students to help you measure the rice with the chosen method, and discuss the findings as a group.

Purpose

Tell students that they will choose the proper tools for measuring various objects. Their job is to decide which tools to use for measuring the objects and to explain their choices.

Input

Collect as many of these measuring tools as possible. Help students identify the tools, and encourage them to provide examples of items that can be measured with each tool. Review with students the correct methods for using different tools.

- Capacity: measuring spoons, measuring cups, and containers in these sizes—pint, liter, half gallon, and gallon
- Weight/Mass: bathroom scale, balance scale, produce scale, and baby scale
- Length: ruler, yardstick, meter stick, and measuring tape
- Time: calendar, stopwatch, clock, and sand timer

Modeling

For deeper understanding of mathematics, the what, the why, and the how must be well connected. Then students can attach importance to different patterns and engage in mathematical reasoning.

Point out several objects, such as a glass of water, a piece of paper, and the classroom door. Ask students how they would measure each object, for example, "If I wanted to know how tall the door was, which tool would I use?" (*yardstick, tape measure, ruler*). "Why shouldn't I use my arm? A measuring cup? A scale?" Allow students to offer reasons why the tool they chose is appropriate for the task. If there is more than one tool that could measure an item, discuss the differences between the tools and the reasons for using each one.

Guided Practice

Organize your measuring tools into four categories—capacity, weight, length, and time. Place each group of tools in a different workstation. Divide the class into four groups, and direct each group to a different workstation. Give students time to examine the tools and practice measuring different items with them. Circulate among the groups, and ask students to demonstrate the correct method for using tools in each workstation. Then have groups rotate through the stations until each group has visited each workstation.

Give students copies of the **Measurement Activity Cards** and **Measurement Record Sheet reproducibles (pages 84–85).** They will choose four activity cards to complete individually or with partners. As they complete each activity, they will record results on the record sheet. Students must choose one activity for each type of measurement—capacity, weight, length, and time. Read aloud each question on the activity cards, and have students mark their choices on their reproducibles.

Checking for Understanding

Be sure that each student chooses one activity for each category. Answer any questions.

Independent Practice

Collect materials listed on the Measurement Activity Cards, and place them in the workstations. Allow students to complete their measurement activities independently or with partners. Remind them to record their results on the record sheet. Then have groups rotate to new workstations. Continue until each group has visited each workstation.

Closure

When students have completed all four measuring activities, ask them to share their results. Discuss why there may be differences between answers for the same activities. For example, various shoes will have different weights based on their sizes and the materials from which they are made (e.g., leather or cotton). Then ask students to respond to the following question in their math journals: "Why do we need different tools to measure different items?"

Name _____   Date _____

Measurement Activity Cards

Directions: Choose one measuring activity for each group.

How many days are there until the next holiday?	How many jumping jacks can you do in 22 seconds?	How many minutes are left before school is over today?	How many animals can you name in 1 minute?
How tall are you?	How long is your arm?	What is the distance between your desk and a window?	How long is a paperclip?
How much does a dictionary weigh?	How much does a trophy weigh?	How much do your shoes weigh?	How much does a box of pencils weigh?
How much rice is in the bag?	How much water can fit in a soda bottle?	How much water can an eye dropper hold?	How much water can a bucket hold?

Measurement Record Sheet

Directions: You visited four measurement workstations. Write what you measured, and describe the results. Write the name of the tool you used. Then explain why it was a good choice for that measurement.

I measured _____ 🕐 _____ My results: _____ _____ I used _____ This was a good choice because _____	I measured _____ 📏 _____ My results: _____ _____ I used _____ This was a good choice because _____
I measured _____ ⚖️ _____ My results: _____ _____ I used _____ This was a good choice because _____	I measured _____ 🥄 _____ My results: _____ _____ I used _____ This was a good choice because _____

MEASURE MANIA

Objectives

Students will use nonstandard measurements to measure the heights of various toys.

Students will describe the benefits of using standard measurements.

Anticipatory Set

Prior to the activity, invite students to bring in one doll or stuffed animal each from home. Assemble the toys on a table at the front of the classroom. Ask students to identify which dolls and animals are the tallest and which are the shortest. Then call on volunteers to group the toys into three categories—short, medium, and tall. Point out two toys and ask, "How much taller is this toy than this one? What kinds of tools can we use to find out?"

Invite two volunteers to make paperclip chains to compare the heights of the two toys. Then call on two more volunteers to use stacks of Unifix cubes to show the height of the two toys. Invite students to compare the two methods of measuring and the results for each.

Purpose

Tell students that they will measure the heights of different toys. They will use nonstandard units of measurement such as paperclips, coins, Unifix cubes, and erasers.

Input

Explain that *nonstandard measurement* means that the items used to measure are not the same size. For example, paperclips come in different sizes, so they would be nonstandard tools of measurement. Make two paperclip chains of the same length, one with large paperclips and one with small paperclips. Point out that both chains are made of paperclips, but the large paperclip chain has fewer units than the small paperclip chain.

Demonstrate how to measure one of the toys with each paperclip chain. Discuss with students why the measurement results differ (*The large paperclip chain needs fewer units than the small paperclip chain.*). Ask students to suggest different nonstandard items that could be used for measuring (e.g., paperclips, coins, shoes, hands, fingers, chalk, crayons, pencils, and erasers).

Modeling

Tell students that they will work in groups to take different measurements of the same toys. Invite four volunteers to help you demonstrate. Copy the **Measure Mania reproducible (page 88)** onto an overhead transparency, and write students' names under the heading "Group Members."

Have one student pick up the toy he or she brought from home and draw a picture of it in the box. Have the student write his or her name in the sentence "This is _____'s toy." Next, tell the four students they will use their pinky fingers to measure the toy's height. Write "our pinkies" to complete the sentence in box 1. Ask student A to record his or her results on the line next to "A" in box 1. Continue, having students B through D measure the toy and record their results.

Then ask the toy's owner to choose another nonstandard tool to measure it. Write the name of that tool (e.g., chalk, coins, erasers) in box 2, and repeat the procedure. Finally, have the toy's owner choose a standard measuring tool, such as a ruler or a tape measure, to measure the height of the toy. Have him or her write the name of the tool used and the results in the sentence frames at the bottom of the page.

Guided Practice

Let students collect their toys and arrange themselves into groups of four. Give students copies of the Measure Mania reproducible. Direct the groups to gather their toys and select one toy to begin. The toy's owner will choose the measuring tools and record the results on his or her reproducible. Circulate around the room to make sure each student in the group is getting a chance to measure the toy using both types of tools.

Checking for Understanding

Make sure that students understand how to measure the toys correctly using nonstandard measuring tools. Answer any questions while students work.

Independent Practice

After completing the Guided Practice activity, allow students to work together to measure the remaining toys in their group. Remind them that the owner of each toy will fill out the reproducible with each group member's results.

Closure

In their groups, invite students to discuss why using standard measurements is more effective than using nonstandard measurements. Ask students to reflect on this activity in their journals. Prompt them with questions such as, *What did you think of this activity? Was it difficult to use nonstandard units of measurement for this task? Why or why not? Do you think it is important to use a standard form of measurement?* and *Why or why not?*

Name _____   Date _____

Measure Mania

Directions: Work with your group to measure a toy. Use nonstandard measurement tools first. Then measure the toy using a standard tool.

Group Members

This is _____'s toy.

A. _____

B. _____

C. _____

D. _____

Draw the toy.

1. We measured this toy with	2. Then we measured with
_____	_____
A. _____ tall.	A. _____ tall.
B. _____ tall.	B. _____ tall.
C. _____ tall.	C. _____ tall.
D. _____ tall.	D. _____ tall.

I used a _____ to find the standard height of

my toy. It is _____ tall.

ME AND MY SHADOW

Objectives

Students will estimate and measure the lengths of their shadows.

Students will graph the results of their shadow measurements.

Anticipatory Set

Hang a sheet of white butcher paper on a wall. Dim the lights in the class-room, and turn on an overhead projector so its light shines on the paper. Invite students to come up and use the projector to make shadow puppets on the wall. Encourage them to experiment with placing their hands closer to or farther away from the light to make the shadows appear larger or smaller.

Purpose

Tell students that they will estimate the lengths of their shadows at different times of the day. They will then measure their shadows to find the actual lengths.

> Ask students to estimate before they measure. This builds a stronger sense of measurement units and what they represent.

Input

Ask students to describe what makes a good estimate (*It is reasonable and possible.*). Then have them brainstorm with partners the different methods for measuring their shadows. Help them realize that they will need to work with partners to make these measurements.

Modeling

Give each student a copy of the **Me and My Shadow reproducible (page 91)** and a clipboard. Take the class outside to a sunny spot. Place a strip of masking tape on the ground, and write your name on it with a permanent marker. Then stand with your heels touching the tape and facing your shadow. Ask students to estimate the length of your shadow. Make your own estimate, and record it on the reproducible.

Then have a student place a second strip of masking tape on the ground at the far end of your shadow. Ask him or her to write your name and the time on the tape. Use a yardstick, meter stick, or tape measure to find the actual length of your shadow, and show students how to record the information on the reproducible.

Guided Practice

Organize students into pairs, and give each pair a roll of masking tape and a marker. Guide them through the process that you demonstrated in the Modeling section. Have students take turns making a shadow and marking the ends of the shadow with tape. Be sure that students estimate the lengths of their shadows before taking the actual measurements. Remind students to record their names and the time on the tape.

Once students have estimated and measured the lengths of their shadows, bring them back together. Ask them to predict whether the length of their shadows will get longer or shorter as the day goes on. Tell them to write their predictions on their reproducibles.

Checking for Understanding

When you return to the classroom, encourage students to share their results from the activity. Listen carefully for any estimates that were far from accurate. Discuss with students how to make more reasonable estimates.

Independent Practice

Bring students outside two more times during the day. Have them work with the same partners and return to their original spots, marked by strips of masking tape. Ask them to repeat the process to both estimate and measure the lengths of their shadows at each time.

Closure

Ask students if their predictions about when their shadows would be the longest were accurate (*Shadows will be longest when the sun is lowest in the sky.*). Then use a bulletin board to create a classroom graph that shows the results of the activity. Mark measurements in 5-inch increments along the left-hand side of the graph. Then divide the space vertically into three sections, and write the times the measurements were taken along the bottom of the graph. Give students lengths of yarn in two colors. Have them use one color to show their estimate and another color to show the true measurement. Tell students to cut the pieces of yarn to the appropriate lengths and attach them to the graph.

Ask students to write about their experiences in their math journals. Prompt students with questions such as, *What happened to your shadow as the day went on? Did it get shorter or longer? Were you surprised? How did your estimates compare to the actual lengths?* and *Did your estimate become more accurate each time?*

Me and My Shadow

Directions: Look at your shadow. Estimate the length, and write it on the line. Then measure your shadow, and record the actual length. Draw clock hands to show the time you took the measurement. Repeat two more times.

My Estimate: _____

Actual Length: _____

My Estimate: _____

Actual Length: _____

My Estimate: _____

Actual Length: _____

TIC-TAC-TIME

Objective

Students will practice telling time to the quarter hour.

Anticipatory Set

Draw a large tic-tac-toe grid on the board. Ask students if they know what it is. Then ask them to tell you the rules for playing tic-tac-toe (*Players choose a symbol such as X or O and take turns writing their symbols on the game board. The first player to get three Xs or Os in a row wins the game.*). Choose a student volunteer to play the game with you using the grid you drew on the board. If time permits, play a few additional games with other students.

Purpose

Tell students that they will practice how to tell time to the quarter hour with a game that is similar to both Tic-Tac-Toe and Bingo.

Input

Use a classroom teaching clock to review telling time to the quarter hour. Invite students to call out the times shown. Ask other students to show how the times are written in numeric form on the board.

Modeling

Copy the **Tic-Tac-Time Clocks reproducibles (pages 94–95)** onto overhead transparencies, and cut out the cards. Shuffle the cards, and place them in a bag. Draw a new tic-tac-toe grid on the board, and ask volunteers to call out different times that show hours, half hours, and quarter hours, such as 2:00, 7:30, 1:15, and 9:45. Write a different time on each space on the grid.

Tell students that you will draw a clock face from the bag and place it on the overhead projector so everyone can see it. If the time shown on the clock is written on the grid, one student will be allowed to cross out that time on the grid. If not, you will move on to another card. When three spaces in a row get crossed out, the game is over. Model how to call out "tic-tac-time" at the end of the game.

Next, show students how to make their own game boards by drawing large grids on drawing paper. Then tell them to write the numeric form of nine times in the spaces on the game boards. They may use only times that show hours, half hours, and quarter hours (e.g., 12:00, 12:15, 12:30, and 12:45).

Checking for Understanding

Check students' game boards to make sure they wrote appropriate times for the game. Remind students to cross off each time as it is called.

Guided Practice

Play a practice game using the transparency cards. Draw one card at a time, and place it on the overhead projector so everyone can see it. Give students a minute to look for that time on their game boards and cross off the space. Continue drawing cards and displaying them until one student has crossed off three spaces in a row on his or her game board. Ask the student to read aloud the three times to determine that all answers are correct.

Independent Practice

After the practice game, divide the class into small groups. Give each group copies of the Tic-Tac-Time Clocks reproducibles. Have them cut out the game cards and place them in a bag. Ask each group to choose one player to be the caller. For the first game, players draw a game board and fill in the times. The caller then draws the cards out of the bag and shows them to the rest of the players, and they mark their game boards. At the end of each game, have players trade game boards and choose a new caller. Allow students to continue playing until everyone has had a turn being the caller.

Closure

After everyone has finished playing the game, have students share the times at which they do different activities, for example, *At 7:00 a.m., I get up to get ready for school. At 6:30 p.m., my family eats dinner together. At 3:30 p.m., I have soccer practice.* Encourage students to draw pictures in their journals showing things they do throughout the day. Then have them draw a clock for each picture that shows the time of day at which the activity typically takes place.

Tic-Tac-Time Clocks

Tic-Tac-Time Clocks

RACE FOR TIME!

Objective

Students will identify times on a display clock.

Anticipatory Set

Have students brainstorm a list of different kinds of races that they know about (e.g., car races, horse races, running races, relay races, potato-sack races). Then divide your class into groups, and challenge each group to design a race that can be held on the school's playground. Encourage students to be creative.

When groups are done designing their races, take the class outside. Ask each group to establish its racecourse. Then let group members race against each other while the rest of the class cheers them on.

Purpose

After each group runs its race, tell students that they will play an indoor racing game. This relay race will have teams compete to see who can look at a clock and identify the time shown the fastest.

Input

Review the parts of a clock, pointing out the hour hand, the minute hand, and the numbers. Ask students what the numbers represent when the hour hand points to them and what they represent when the minute hand points to them. As a class, skip count by fives while moving clockwise around the clock from 1 to 12. Then display a few times on the clock, and call on volunteers to identify the times.

Modeling

Copy the **Race for Time! Track reproducible (page 98)** onto an overhead transparency, and place it on the overhead projector. Place two different-colored chips at the start line, and point out the finish line. Divide the class into two teams, and have each team line up single file facing the projector screen. Explain that each team will move its chip forward around the track as players identify the time shown on a display clock. Place a bell or buzzer in front of each team.

Tell students that you will set a time on your classroom display clock and show it to them. The first two students in line will have the chance to ring the bell or buzzer if they can identify the time shown. You will determine who rang in first and give that student a chance to answer. If the student is correct, he or she moves the team's chip one space forward on the track. If he or she is incorrect, the other student gets a chance to give the time. Both students then go to the end of the line, and the next two students in line get a turn.

Play a practice round with the students. Make sure they don't call out answers or give clues to their teammates. The only student who should be talking is the one who rings in first to answer. Continue playing until one team reaches the finish line.

Guided Practice

Divide the class into smaller groups, and give each group a copy of the reproducible. Allow groups to arrange themselves into two teams and select a monitor for their race. The monitor determines which team rings in first and listens for the correct answer. Give each team a colored chip and a bell or buzzer, and let them race against each other as you continue to display times on the clock for the whole class. At the end of the playing period, give the players on each winning team a small token or prize, such as a pencil, eraser, or inexpensive toy.

Checking for Understanding

Gather students together as a group, and show them various times on the display clock. Invite them to shout out the time shown. Take note of students who get times correct and those who make errors. Offer additional help to those who are still having trouble.

Independent Practice

Set up a learning center in your classroom so that small groups of students can play this game independently. Stock the center with a display clock, copies of the Race for Time! Track reproducible, bells or buzzers, and game chips. Encourage students to think of their own race-themed time games as well.

Closure

Ask students to respond to the following question in their math journals: "Why is it important to be able to tell time on an analog clock as well as a digital clock?"

Name _____   Date _____

Race for Time! Track

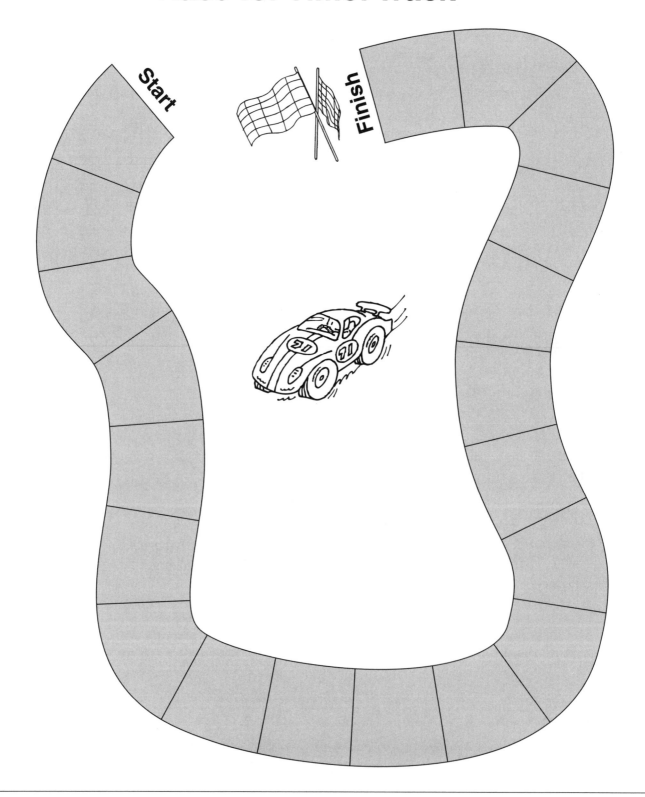

POUR IT OUT

Objective

Students will estimate and measure volume.

Anticipatory Set

Gather five bottles or other containers (two with different shapes but the same volume) and several measuring cups. Fill the containers with water. Make a big show of putting a drop cloth or plastic bags on the floor under a small table or desk that you have placed at the front of the room. Add extra fun and expectation by putting on a raincoat and hat. Tell students, "We'll be working with water today!"

To prepare students for working with volume, hold up several empty containers, such as a large can, a juice carton, a milk jug, and a plastic storage container. Point out that even though the containers are all different shapes, they might hold the same amount (or volume) of liquid. A short, wide container may hold the same amount as a tall, thin container. Ask students to guess which container they think can hold the most liquid and which can hold the least.

Purpose

Tell students that they will be using the bottles and measuring cups to estimate and then measure volume.

Input

Ask students to explain what the term *volume* means and what it measures. After allowing students time to respond to and discuss the concept, explain that volume measures the amount of liquid (or other matter) a container is able to hold.

Modeling

Give students copies of the **Volume Record Sheet reproducible (page 101).** Place the bottles side by side on a table at the front of the room. Label the bottles "A," "B," "C," "D," and "E." Ask students to predict which bottle can hold the most water (has the greatest volume). Tell them to circle their prediction on the reproducible and write a sentence explaining why they chose that container. Record the class predictions on the board.

Then ask students which bottle they think can hold the least water (has the smallest volume). Have them circle this prediction on their reproducible as well. Finally, ask students if they think any of the bottles might have the same volume. Have them indicate on the reproducible which two they think can hold the same amount of water and why.

Tell students that they will be exploring their predictions by pouring water from the bottles into the measuring cups and recording the volume of each bottle. Demonstrate by pouring some water from one container into a measuring cup.

Guided Practice

Ask a volunteer to come to the front of the room and pour water from bottle A into the measuring cups and read the measurements for the rest of the class. Have students record this information on their reproducibles. Dump the water from the measuring cup into a bucket or sink. Call on another volunteer to pour the water from bottle B into measuring cups, and have the class record that amount. Repeat this process until all of the measurements have been taken and recorded.

During the activity, make sure students pour water slowly so they don't spill it. If you wish, give students aprons to wear to protect their clothing.

Checking for Understanding

Check that students understand estimation and volume by initiating a discussion about the activity. Ask questions such as, *Did any of these measurements surprise you? Whose estimations were correct? Whose estimations were incorrect? Why do you think you made incorrect estimations?* and *What did you learn about volume from measuring each bottle and comparing the measurements?*

Closure

Take a few minutes to discuss the importance of measuring versus judging based on the size of the container. Have students complete the Reflections portion of their reproducibles. Ask them to copy this portion of the activity into their math journals for future reference.

Name _____   Date _____

Volume Record Sheet

Directions: Write your estimates, observations, and reflections below.

Estimates

1. Which bottle do you think holds the most water?   A   B   C   D   E

   Why? _____

2. Which bottle do you think holds the least water?   A   B   C   D   E

   Why? _____

3. Which two bottles do you think hold the same   A   B   C   D   E
   amount of water?

   Why? _____

Observations

1. Volume for Bottle A: _____

2. Volume for Bottle B: _____

3. Volume for Bottle C: _____

4. Volume for Bottle D: _____

5. Volume for Bottle E: _____

Reflections

Think about the activity. On the back of this paper, write a short paragraph explaining your thoughts. Below are some questions to get you started. Feel free to add your own ideas.

- What did you learn about measuring volume?

- Does the shape of the bottle matter?

- Did anything surprise you? Why?

MEASUREMENT SCAVENGER HUNT

Objective

Students will estimate and measure perimeter and area.

Anticipatory Set

Before beginning this activity, write a list of objects in and around the classroom and school grounds that students could easily measure for perimeter and area, such as a four-square court, a book, a desktop, a basketball court, a picnic tabletop or bench, a window, a door, the chalkboard, a sidewalk square, and so on. Mark each spot with a special symbol, such as a blue star drawn with sidewalk chalk or a sticky note. Measure each object to make an answer key. You may decide to measure the objects using both metric and customary units. Then reorder your list for each group of four students so that groups won't be measuring the same object at the same time.

Ask students if they have ever gone on a scavenger hunt. Invite them to share their experiences and explain how a scavenger hunt works.

Purpose

Tell students that they will be going on a scavenger hunt to practice measuring area and perimeter. They will then apply that knowledge to the next activity in which they will find the approximate area and perimeter of a much larger object, the classroom.

Input

Explain that *perimeter* is the measurement around the outside of something and *area* is the measurement of the total surface of something. Place a transparency of inch grid paper on the overhead projector. Trace the outside of the grid, and explain that this measurement is perimeter. Then point out all the grid squares inside the grid. Explain that these squares each measure one inch. They make up the area, or entire surface, of the grid.

Modeling

Draw a large rectangle on the grid transparency. Tell students that you will find the perimeter of the shape first. Label the sides "a," "b," "c," and "d." Measure each side, writing its measurement along the edge in inches. Tell students that to get the perimeter, you must add all four sides' measurements. The formula for perimeter is $P = a + b + c + d$. Write the formula on the board, plugging in the inch measurements for your rectangle (e.g., $P = 4$ in. $+ 6$ in. $+ 4$ in. $+ 6$ in.). Ask a volunteer to supply the answer, 20 inches. Point out that if the shape had more than four sides (e.g., six), the formula would be different, such as $P = a + b + c + d + e + f$.

Explain that you will use your perimeter measurements to find the area of the rectangle. Write the formula for area on the board: "A = length (l) × width (w)." Plug in the numbers from your perimeter measurements, and write the answer in square inches: "A = 4 in. × 6 in.," or "A = 24 square inches." Ask students how they can verify the answer (*Count the squares inside the rectangle.*).

Guided Practice

Trace several more rectangles or other polygons on the grid paper transparency, and invite students to help you calculate the perimeter and area of each shape. Encourage students to count grid squares to verify the answers.

Checking for Understanding

Bring students' attention back to the formulas for perimeter and area on the overhead. Then ask students to point to several items in the classroom, such as a desktop or a sheet of paper, and identify how they would measure for perimeter and area.

Independent Practice

Divide the class into groups of four. Distribute the scavenger hunt lists, and tell students that they have 30 minutes to find and measure all the objects on the list. Emphasize that they must measure the objects in the order they appear so groups don't end up at the same object at the same time. Give each group rulers and/or meter sticks, depending on whether you want students to focus on customary or metric measurements. When a group has measured one object, the group should check it off the list and record the measurement. Remind students to record area in square units.

You may want to enlist a parent or a teacher aide to help with this activity. That way, someone can be in the classroom and someone can be outside to guide and assist students as needed.

Closure

When time is up, gather students back in the classroom. Ask each group to share its measurements with the class. Discuss any discrepancies and what might have caused results to differ. Invite each group to explain its methods for measuring each object. Then ask students to write in their math journals about how knowing perimeter and area could help someone decide how much paint to use to paint his or her home or how much carpet to buy for his or her floors.

MEASURE MY CLASSROOM

Objective

Students will determine the perimeters and areas of the classrooms in their school to calculate the square footage of carpeting needed to carpet them.

Anticipatory Set

Before beginning the activity, clear out the edges of your classroom as much as possible to give students the chance to move around freely. Use a sheet of paper and a marker to label each wall, from "A" through "D." Gain students' attention by telling them to imagine the school is installing new carpet in all the classrooms. Their class is responsible for finding out how many square feet of carpet will be needed for the job. Ask students to estimate the size of their class-room in both perimeter and area.

Purpose

Tell students that they will use their knowledge of perimeter and area to determine the size of their classroom. Remind them how they measured the perimeter and area of various objects in the Measurement Scavenger Hunt activity. Explain that they can use these same methods to measure a much larger shape—their classroom.

Input

Review with students the difference between perimeter and area. Ask students if they remember the formulas and how to calculate each measure-ment. Remind them that to find perimeter, they must measure all of the sides and add them together ($P = a + b + c + d$). To find the area, they must multiply the length by the width ($A = l \times w$). Reinforce learning by measuring a com-mon classroom object, such as a book or a desktop. First, measure the sides to get the perimeter. Then multiply the length by the width to get the area.

Modeling

Use meter sticks or yardsticks to measure the width of the chalkboard or whiteboard. Show students how to place the measuring tools end to end, and ask a volunteer to hold them in place as you continue to measure. Measure the height of the board using the same technique. Use your measurements to cal-culate and record the area and the perimeter of the board.

Guided Practice

Divide the class into groups of three or four. Distribute rulers, meter sticks, or yardsticks and the **Carpeting the Classrooms reproducible (page 106)** to each group. Assign each group to a different wall to begin the activity (wall

A, B, C, or D). Spend time with each group, making sure students are using the measuring tools correctly to find the most accurate measurement possible. To make measuring faster and easier, point out that many people use measuring tape for longer measurements. After students have used rulers or meter sticks, work with each group to use measuring tape to verify the measurement. After measuring the first wall, students will move to the next wall in a round-robin fashion until each group has measured all the walls.

Checking for Understanding

Make sure students understand that each group will measure all four walls. Circulate around the room, and offer assistance as needed. Make sure students measure using a ruler, meter stick, or yardstick and then a measuring tape.

> Explore every opportunity for students to see the practical applications of mathematics.

Independent Practice

Have groups continue measuring the outer edges of the classroom, wall by wall, and recording their findings. When they have measured and recorded measurements for all of the walls, have the groups calculate the perimeter and the area of the room. Have them use these and the other classroom measurements shown on the reproducible to calculate the square footage needed to carpet all the classrooms. Allow students to use calculators.

Closure

Gather everyone back together as one large group, and invite students to share their findings. Are their measurements all the same? Discuss with students how they could end up with variations in measurement. Invite them to share how they could be more accurate. Afterward, ask students to write the most important thing they learned during this activity in their math journals.

Carpeting the Classrooms

Directions: Measure each wall of your classroom. Record the measurements, and then calculate the perimeter and area. Then calculate the cost of carpet for each classroom.

Carpet is $2.50 per square foot.

My Classroom

Wall A: _____

Wall B: _____

Wall C: _____

Wall D: _____

Perimeter: _____

Area: _____

Miss Chang's Classroom

45 ft

25 ft [   ] 25 ft

45 ft

Perimeter: _____

Area: _____

Cost of carpet: _____

Miss Griffith's Classroom

39 ft

32 ft [   ] 32 ft

39 ft

Perimeter: _____

Area: _____

Cost of carpet: _____

Mrs. Garcia's Classroom

40 ft

27 ft [   ] 27 ft

40 ft

Perimeter: _____

Area: _____

Cost of carpet: _____

Mr. Green's Classroom

34 ft

35 ft [   ] 35 ft

34 ft

Perimeter: _____

Area: _____

Cost of carpet: _____

Mrs. Owen's Classroom

48 ft

23 ft [   ] 23 ft

48 ft

Perimeter: _____

Area: _____

Cost of carpet: _____

Square Footage of All Classrooms: _____

Cost of Carpeting All Classrooms: _____

BOX IT!

Objective

Students will measure boxes for volume to find out how much can fit inside of them.

Anticipatory Set

Before beginning the activity, gather seven different-sized boxes. (Make sure to have at least one cube.) Number six of the boxes, from "1" through "6," and display them for the class. Set aside the extra box to use during Modeling and Guided Practice.

Ask students to name a variety of uses for boxes, such as packing, storing, and shipping items. Ask students what they might pack in a small box (e.g., toys, books) and what they might pack in a large box (e.g., appliances, clothing). Ask students, "How might we find out how much will fit inside these boxes? How can we measure these boxes?"

Purpose

Tell students that they will work in small groups to determine how much space is inside each box. This space is called *volume.*

Input

Remind students that perimeter is the measurement around the outside of something and area is the measurement of the total surface of something. Show your extra box to students. Point out the outline of the box, and explain that that is the perimeter. Then point to the bottom surface of the box, and explain that this is the area. Finally, point to the inside of the box, and explain that this is the volume. Volume is the measurement of the space inside of an object, such as a ball, bottle, pool, balloon, or box.

Place several items inside the box, such as books. Tell students that determining the volume of the box can help them find out how many books will fit inside.

Modeling

Explain that just like with perimeter and area, there is a formula for calculating the volume of an object. The formula for volume differs depending on the shape of the object. Because boxes are usually cubes or rectangular prisms, the formula for volume is V = length × width × height (or V = lwh). Write the formula on the board.

Point out each edge of the box that shows the length, the width, and the height. Use a ruler or meter stick to measure each edge, and write the measurements on the board, for example, "Length = 8 inches, Width = 5 inches,

Height = 10 inches." Then plug the numbers into the formula: "V = 8 in. × 5 in. × 10 in.," or "V = 400 cubic inches."

Point out that if the box were a perfect cube, the length, width, and height all would be the same. Students would simply multiply the length or the width or the height by itself three times, or cube it. For example, if the width were 8 inches, then the calculation would be $V = 8^3$, or V = 512 cubic inches.

Guided Practice

Divide the class into six mixed-ability groups. Give each group a copy of the **Box It! Record Sheet reproducible (page 109)** and one of the numbered boxes. As you go from group to group, use your extra box to guide them through the steps for measuring volume. Tell each group to measure the length, then the width, then the height. Have them multiply their measurements to get the volume for each box.

Checking for Understanding

As groups complete their measurements for their first boxes, circulate around the room, and make sure that they understand the difference between measuring for perimeter, area, and volume. Invite a volunteer to describe how to measure for each one.

Independent Practice

Have each group pass the box that it measured to the group on its right. Each group then takes the box from the group on its left. Have students repeat the measuring task for the second box. They should continue in this manner until all six groups have measured all six boxes.

Closure

Invite groups to compare their measurements of the six boxes. If measurements are different, encourage students to discuss their measuring methods. Then ask students to write in their journals how knowing the volume of a box or other object (such as a pool or bathtub) might be helpful in certain situations. Have them record the formulas for perimeter, area, and volume.

Extend the Activity

Challenge students to measure the volume of a book or other geometric object to find out how many books would fit inside a given box.

Name _____   Date _____

Box It! Record Sheet

Directions: Find the volume of each box. Write the measurements below.

1
Length: _____
Width: _____
Height: _____
Volume: _____

4
Length: _____
Width: _____
Height: _____
Volume: _____

2
Length: _____
Width: _____
Height: _____
Volume: _____

5
Length: _____
Width: _____
Height: _____
Volume: _____

3
Length: _____
Width: _____
Height: _____
Volume: _____

6
Length: _____
Width: _____
Height: _____
Volume: _____

109

6

Geometry

NAME MY SHAPE

Objective

Students will identify two- and three-dimensional shapes based on descriptions from a partner.

Anticipatory Set

Choose a simple photograph or illustration from a magazine. Keep the image out of students' view. Describe the picture to students as they attempt to draw a picture that matches your description. Encourage them to keep their drawings out of view from classmates until the picture is complete.

When you have finished describing the picture, hold it up so everyone can see it. Have students compare their drawings to the magazine picture and discuss the differences between them. Invite students to offer ideas as to how your descriptions could be changed to make their drawings more accurately match the magazine picture.

Purpose

Tell students that they will draw and identify shapes based on descriptions given by partners.

Input

Collect a variety of two- and three-dimensional shapes. Hold up one shape at a time, and review its name and attributes with students. Call on volunteers to provide descriptions of different shapes while classmates try to guess the names of the shapes being described.

Modeling

Draw an isosceles triangle on a sheet of paper. Hide the paper so students cannot see it. Then describe the shape you drew as students try to replicate it on drawing paper. Describe the shape, for example, "My shape has three sides and three angles. One of my shape's angles is at the top of my paper, and the other two are at the bottom. The bottom side of my shape is shorter than the two slanted sides."

Give students time to draw the shape you described. Then have them label their drawings. Show your drawing of the triangle, and check to see if everyone has drawn a triangle similar to yours.

Guided Practice

Give each student a clipboard and several sheets of drawing paper. Divide the class into pairs, and have each pair sit back to back. Direct one student from each pair to secretly draw a shape on a piece of paper and describe it to his or her partner. Ask the other student to attempt to draw a matching picture as the shape is described. When the drawings are complete, have partners label their pictures with the shape's name. Then allow partners to compare their two pictures.

Checking for Understanding

Give each pair a chance to share its pictures with the class and discuss how well the pictures match. If the pictures do not match, invite partners to explain what they could have done differently to create a better match.

Independent Practice

Allow plenty of time for students to repeat the activity several times. Have them take several turns in each role, as both the describer and the listener. Encourage partners to draw both two- and three-dimensional shapes. Circulate around the room and listen closely to students' verbal descriptions. Make note of any students who are having difficulty so you can provide additional instruction.

Closure

Invite students to spend 2 minutes talking to their partners about this activity. They should discuss what made a good description and what made a poor description. Then ask students to draw a two-dimensional shape and a three-dimensional shape in their math journals. Have them write a description of each shape next to the drawings.

SHAPE STORIES

Objectives

Students will identify shapes in the environment.

Students will identify shapes in a story.

Students will write stories about shapes.

Anticipatory Set

Take students outside to the playground, and tell them that they are going on a Shape Scavenger Hunt. Give students a copy of the **Shape Cards reproducible (page 116).** Then provide them with 10 minutes to find as many shapes shown on the cards as they can. Encourage them to search around the buildings and play structures to find the shapes. They can make notes on their reproducibles to help them remember where they saw each shape. When you return to the classroom, allow volunteers to share their observations with the class.

> Making the task relevant, interesting, and significant invites students to care and, consequently, invites them to engage in mathematics.

Purpose

Tell students that they will listen to a story about a triangle and then they will write their own stories about a shape.

Input

Read aloud *The Greedy Triangle* by Marilyn Burns. Discuss what the triangle loves about being a triangle. Then have students recall the different shapes that the triangle becomes. Discuss with students where different shapes appear in our environment. For example, windows are often rectangles or squares, and stop signs are octagons.

Modeling

Copy the **Shape Story Planner reproducible (page 117)** onto a transparency, and place it on the overhead projector. Tell students that you will work together to plan and write a class story about a square. Draw and label a square in the box at the top of the reproducible. Then point out the two headings on the story planner—"Place My Shape Is Found" and "Why My Shape Likes This Place."

Ask volunteers to think of places where squares can be found (*windows, library books, sandwiches*). Record their responses in the square shapes. Then ask volunteers to suggest why a square would be happy in each of these places, and record the responses in the rectangles (*As a window, a square can see all the fun things families do together in their homes. As a library book, a square can lose itself in a good story. As a sandwich, a square can hear all of a child's best jokes during lunchtime.*). After the Shape Story Planner is complete, suggest that students help you turn the notes into a short story titled "The Happy Square."

Guided Practice

Invite each student to select a shape from the Shape Cards reproducible, and give students a copy of the Shape Story Planner. Direct them to draw and label the shape they chose in the box at the top of the page. Then guide them to describe one place the shape can be found and why the shape would enjoy being in that place.

Checking for Understanding

Ask each student to share the first section of his or her story planner. Make sure students understand that they are listing places where the shapes can be found and what the shapes would like about those places.

Independent Practice

Have students finish filling out their story planners independently. Then have them write and illustrate their stories.

Closure

Have students find partners and read aloud their stories to each other. Compile all the completed stories into a class book titled *Our Happy Shapes.* Then ask students to write in their math journals about the different shapes they see in the world around them.

Name _____   **Date** _____

  # Shape Cards

Directions: Go on a Shape Scavenger Hunt! Find as many of these shapes as you can.

circle	square
triangle	rectangle
rhombus	hexagon
pentagon	octagon

Name _____ **Date** _____

Shape Story Planner

Directions: Use this story planner to help you write a story about a shape.

My Shape

Place My Shape Is Found   Why My Shape Likes This Place

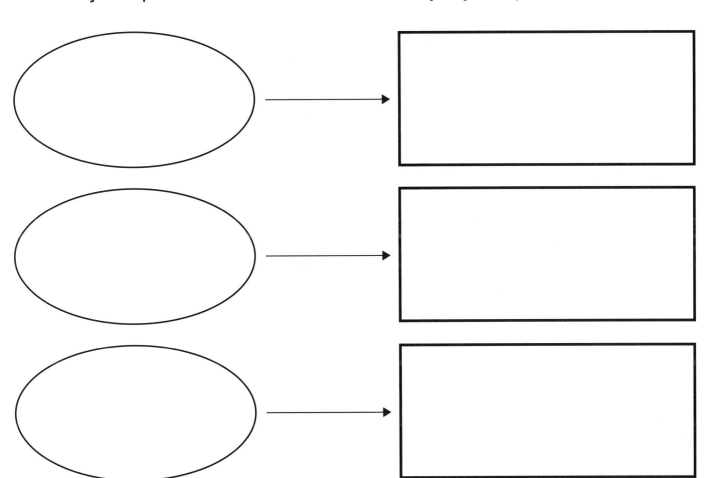

SHAPE-Y SHAKE-Y

Objective

Students will identify three-dimensional shapes.

Anticipatory Set

Ask students if they have ever danced to "The Hokey Pokey." Ask everyone to stand up and dance a round of the song. Sing, "You put your right foot in. You put your right foot out. You put your right foot in, and you shake it all about. You do the Hokey Pokey, and you turn yourself around. That's what it's all about!" Invite students to sing along with you and dance to several more verses.

Purpose

Tell students that they will practice identifying shapes with a song and dance similar to "The Hokey Pokey."

Input

Copy the **Shape-y Shake-y Cards reproducible (page 120)** onto cardstock for yourself and your students. With students, cut out the cards, and glue or tape a craft stick to the back of each card. Hold up your cards, one at a time, and have students find and hold up matching cards. Ask volunteers to name the shapes and describe their attributes.

Modeling

Tell students that you will show them how to do a dance by choosing a practice shape. Pick up your pyramid card and sing, "You put your pyramid in. You put your pyramid out. You put your pyramid in, and you shake it all about. You do the Shape-y Shake-y, and you turn yourself around. That's what it's all about!" Act silly when you dance, and clap three times at the end.

Guided Practice

Tell students that they will repeat the song for each of their card shapes. Have them spread out around the classroom and place their cards faceup on the floor at their feet. Invite one student to select a shape and call out its name. Give the class a moment to find the corresponding shape card, and sing the verse together as students dance with their shapes. When the verse is over, have students place the shape card facedown on the floor. Choose another student to select the next shape, and continue singing different verses until all of the shapes have been used.

Checking for Understanding

As students dance to the song, check that they are showing the correct shapes. Note any students who are having trouble. When time permits, give them additional practice identifying three-dimensional shapes.

Independent Practice

Have students complete the **Shape-y Shake-y Practice reproducible (page 121).** Instruct them to write the names of the shapes on the lines. Create an answer key by completing a reproducible and stapling it into a construction paper folder. Encourage students to check their own work against the answer key.

Closure

Have students choose partners. Tell partners to take turns describing a three-dimensional shape and guessing which shape is being described. Encourage them to include descriptions of items that have that shape. For example, to describe a cube, a student might say, "I am the shape of a game die," or "I am the shape of an ice cube."

Then suggest that students copy and complete this sentence frame in their math journals: "I am a _____ [name of three-dimensional shape]. I am the shape of _____ [name of object that has this shape]." Have them draw pictures of the shape and the object to accompany the sentence.

Shape-y Shake-y Cards

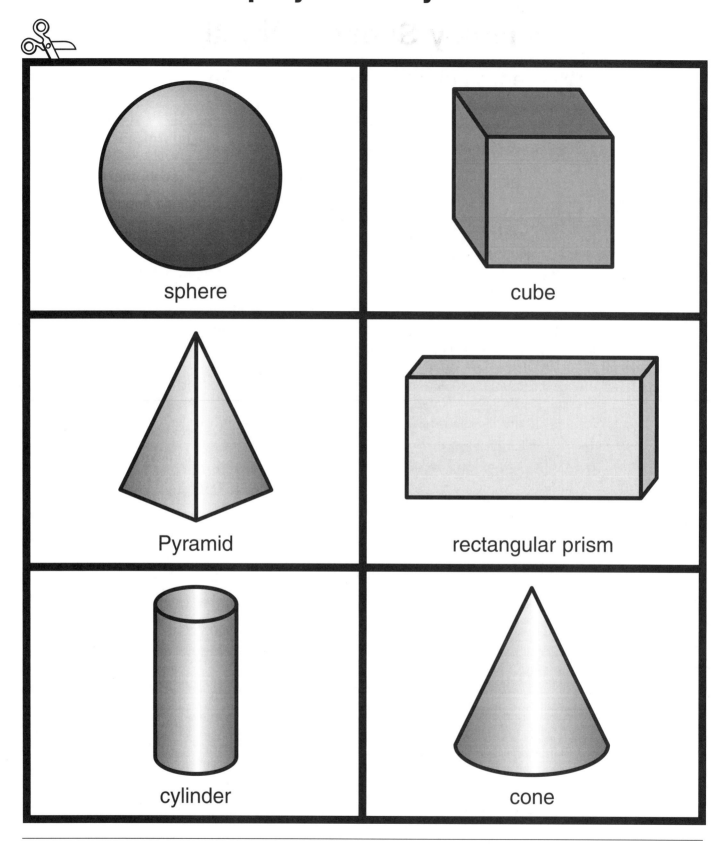

sphere

cube

Pyramid

rectangular prism

cylinder

cone

Shape-y Shake-y Practice

Directions: Choose a word from the box, and write it under the correct shape.

sphere	cube
pyramid	rectangular prism
cylinder	cone

1.

_____

2.

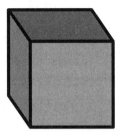

_____

3.

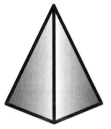

_____

4.

_____

5.

_____

6.

_____

PATTERN BLOCK PARTY

Objective

Students will create patterns using pattern blocks.

Anticipatory Set

Clap your hands together to make a sound pattern. Invite students to clap along with you to extend the pattern. Make new sound patterns with different sounds, such as snapping, stomping, and whistling. Invite volunteers to create their own patterns, and invite the class join in.

Then ask students to look around the classroom for visual patterns. Encourage them to discover patterns on clothes, bulletin board displays, and various classroom objects. Have each student describe one pattern to the class without identifying the object. Students should note shapes and colors found in the pattern. Challenge the class to identify the object with the pattern each student describes.

> Ask students to use concrete objects whenever possible, such as counting each type of bean in a mixture or the number of marbles of each color in a collection.

Purpose

Tell students that they will use pattern blocks to build simple and complex patterns. They will then exchange patterns with a partner and see if they can identify and extend the new pattern.

Input

Hold up pattern blocks, one at a time, and ask students to identify the shapes. Encourage students to describe the shape's attributes as well. For example, a hexagon has six equal sides and six equal angles. In a pattern block set, the hexagon is usually yellow.

Modeling

Place several pattern blocks on the overhead projector, and arrange them into a simple AB pattern, such as orange square, green triangle, orange square, green triangle. Invite a volunteer to use pattern blocks to extend the pattern that you started. Continue making patterns, and increase the complexity as you progress. Create some patterns using a straight line, and create others that fill a broader space. As students work with you to extend the patterns, encourage them to describe the attributes of the shapes used and their relationships to one another.

Guided Practice

Give each student several sheets of white paper along with a set of pattern blocks and colored pencils or crayons. Direct students to place the pattern blocks on the white paper to create patterns in varying degrees of difficulty. Then have them trace the blocks and color in the shapes on the paper. Ask students to exchange papers with partners and use blocks to extend the patterns colored on the paper.

Checking for Understanding

Circulate around the room to see if each student is creating a repeating pattern that can be duplicated. Periodically call on one student at a time to describe the pattern he or she is creating.

Independent Practice

Suggest that students use their remaining sheets of paper to create pictures using the pattern blocks that incorporate different patterns. Have them trace only the outline of their completed pictures with a crayon or marker. Individual blocks should not be drawn or colored in. Collect all the pictures, and then redistribute them so each student has someone else's picture. Challenge students to use the pattern blocks to re-create the original pictures.

Closure

Ask students to describe the ways that different blocks can be combined to make a new shape. For example, two trapezoids can be combined to create a hexagon, and two triangles can create a square.

Have students draw pattern block patterns in their math journals. Encourage them to write sentences to describe the patterns.

LETTER PERFECT SYMMETRY

Objective

Students will recognize and demonstrate lines of symmetry.

Anticipatory Set

Before the lesson, prepare a set of letter cards for every two students. Photocopy the **Letter Symmetry Cards reproducibles (pages 126–127),** and cut out the cards. Place each set of cards in a resealable plastic bag.

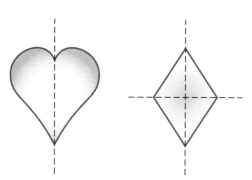

Show students several simple pictures that have various lines of symmetry. Show a picture of a heart, and explain that it has one line of symmetry. Point to the line. Show examples of other objects that have one, two, three, or even four lines of symmetry. Point out that if each of these objects were folded in half, each side, or half, would be identical.

Purpose

Tell students that they will be using alphabet letter cards to demonstrate lines of symmetry.

Input

Reinforce learning by asking a volunteer to explain the meaning of *line of symmetry* and *symmetrical.* Remind students that when a shape (such as a letter) has a line of symmetry, it means that you could fold the shape or cut it in half and the two halves would be exactly the same size and shape. When two objects are exactly the same size and shape, they are called *symmetrical* or *congruent.*

Modeling

Draw a large capital letter *A* on the board. Ask students if this letter is symmetrical. Explain that it is symmetrical only if you draw a line of symmetry from the top point all the way down in a vertical line. The left and right sides would be identical. Demonstrate by drawing a line down the middle of the letter, from top to bottom. Ask students if there is another line of symmetry (*no*). Point out that if you draw a line horizontally across the middle of the letter, the upper and lower parts of the *A* are not symmetrical. Draw this line on the board, and point out the two different parts.

Guided Practice

Next, draw a capital letter *B* on the board. Invite students to write a large capital letter *B* on a sheet of paper and follow along during your demonstration. Ask students if the letter *B* is symmetrical and to identify its line of symmetry (*horizontal*). Draw the line of symmetry on the board while students follow along on their paper. Invite them to fold their paper in half on the line and identify if both the top and bottom of the *B* are symmetrical (*yes*). Ask volunteers to try to find another line of symmetry. Students will discover that there is only one line of symmetry for the letter *B*.

Independent Practice

Give each pair of students a bag of letter cards and a copy of the **Letter Symmetry Record Sheet reproducible (page 128).** Tell students that they will work with partners to explore the other capital letters of the alphabet to find out if they are symmetrical and to identify their lines of symmetry. Point out that the answers for the letters *A* and *B* have already been completed. They will record the rest of their findings.

Closure

Have students work individually to discover how many lines of symmetry they can find in the letters of their first and last names. Ask them to record their results in their math journals.

Letter Symmetry Cards

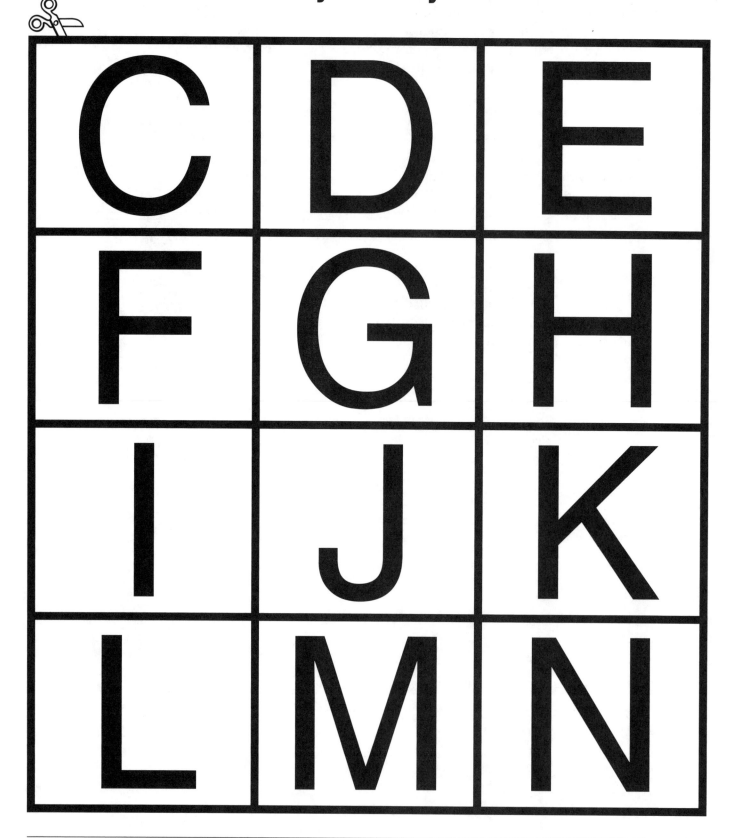

C	D	E
F	G	H
I	J	K
L	M	N

Letter Symmetry Cards

O	P	Q
R	S	T
U	V	W
X	Y	Z

127

Letter Symmetry Record Sheet

Directions: Look at each letter card. Is the letter symmetrical? Write **yes** or **no.** Then record the number of lines of symmetry and the directions of the lines (**horizontal or vertical**). **A** and **B** are done for you.

Letter	Symmetrical?	How Many Lines?	Line Directions
A	Yes	1	Vertical
B	Yes	1	Horizontal
C			
D			
E			
F			
G			
H			
I			
J			
K			
L			
M			
N			
O			
P			
Q			
R			
S			
T			
U			
V			
W			
X			
Y			
Z			

WE'RE CONGRUENT

Objective

Students will demonstrate an understanding of congruency.

Anticipatory Set

Gather a set of attribute blocks for the activity. Copy the **We're Congruent! reproducible (page 131)** onto a transparency so you can demonstrate the activity on the overhead projector. Then photocopy and distribute the reproducible to each student.

Have each student select four attribute blocks and trace one in each of the four quadrants on the reproducible. Select and copy four attribute blocks onto the transparency, and place it on the overhead projector. Collect the attribute blocks, and have students set aside their reproducibles.

Invite students to look around the room and identify the different shapes they see. Point out items such as the clock (circle), a book (rectangle), TV screen (square), and so on. Have them identify attribute blocks with the same shapes.

Purpose

Tell students that they will be using different shapes to demonstrate congruency.

Input

Ask students to recall that congruency is when one figure is exactly the same size and shape as another figure. Hold up two attribute blocks that are the same shape but different sizes. Ask students if the shapes are congruent (*no*). Next, hold up two blocks that are same size but different shapes. Ask students if the shapes are congruent (*no*). Finally, hold up two shapes that are the same size and shape but different colors. Ask students if the shapes are congruent (*yes*). Ask students to identify why these shapes are congruent if they are different colors (*They are the same shape and size.*).

Modeling

Tell students that they will be going on a "congruency hunt." They will trace attribute blocks on activity sheets and then find classmates with congruent shapes. The goal is to find a classmate for each shape and write that student's name in the box.

Place your copy of the reproducible activity sheet on the overhead projector. Point to one of the shapes, and ask if anyone in the room has a congruent shape. Choose one student to bring his or her paper to you. Check to make sure the shapes are congruent, and have that student write his or her name in the box next to that shape. Students will follow this process for each of their shapes.

Once they have found a name for all four shapes, students should sit back down at their desks.

Checking for Understanding

Ask students if they have any questions. Clear up any confusion or misunderstandings before they get out of their seats to hunt for congruent shapes. Remind students that congruent shapes must be the same size and shape.

Independent Practice

Invite students to walk around the room with their activity sheets and pencils to try to find other students with congruent shapes. Make sure students with congruent shapes sign each other's papers. If students are having trouble identifying whether shapes are congruent, prompt them with clues to guide their decision: "Are the shapes the same size?" "Are they the same shape?" and "Do these shapes have the same number of sides and angles?"

Closure

After the activity, ask students to draw and label several congruent shapes in their math journals. Have them place their completed activity sheets inside their math folders. The next time you need to pair students for an activity, you might partner each one with someone who wrote his or her name on the activity sheet.

We're Congruent!

Directions: Trace a shape block in each box below. Find a student with a congruent shape. Have each student sign his or her name in the matching box.

Name: _____	Name: _____
Name: _____	Name: _____

POLYGON ART

Objective

Students will combine polygons to create new polygons in the form of artwork.

Anticipatory Set

Ahead of time, gather a set of pattern blocks for this activity. Explain that a polygon is a closed shape made of line segments, such as a square, a rectangle, a triangle, a circle, and so on. Ask students to think of common polygons they see in the world around them (e.g., stop sign—pentagon, clock—circle, yield sign—triangle, chalkboard—rectangle). Then ask them to close their eyes and imagine a world without polygons. There would be no buildings, no cars, no bikes. . . . Things would look very different.

> The more connections we make through creative and analytical processes, the stronger and longer lasting memory is likely to be.

Purpose

Tell students that they will use pattern blocks to create their own piece of artwork. They will form new polygons by putting common polygons together.

Input

Reinforce learning by asking a volunteer to explain the meaning of *polygon*. Remind students that a polygon is a closed shape made of line segments. Ask students, "What is a three-sided polygon called?" (*triangle*). "What are some four-sided polygons?" (*rectangle, square, rhombus*).

Modeling

Place a pattern block on the overhead projector. This does not need to be a pattern block designed for the overhead; the shadow of the opaque block will show perfectly. Ask students to identify the shape. Then place a different-shaped block next to the first block. Ask students to identify that shape as well. Place the two shapes together to form a new shape. Ask students to count the number of sides and angles on the new polygon.

Trace around your new shape with an overhead marker. Explain that when they put together pattern blocks to form new polygons, they will be placing them on their paper and tracing around them to form different shapes for their artwork.

Guided Practice

Distribute a handful of pattern blocks, several sheets of construction paper, pencils, crayons or markers, scissors, and glue to each student. Use a new transparency and marker to trace several shapes in an artistic pattern. Ask students to follow your lead by beginning to lay out their artwork on the construction paper.

Invite students to use the blocks to form new polygons. Encourage them to lay out and trace their designs in pencil before finalizing their designs with crayons or markers. Students may also wish to trace and cut out different polygons from colored construction paper and make a creative collage.

Checking for Understanding

Make sure students understand that they are to use existing polygons (from the pattern blocks) to create new polygons for their artwork. Walk around the classroom, and randomly ask students to identify and name the polygons represented by the pattern blocks. Answer any questions, and guide student work as needed.

Independent Practice

Invite students to complete their artwork. Encourage them to be as creative and original as possible, using cool and warm colors, complementary colors, and repeating patterns.

Closure

Gather students together into a large group, and invite them to share their artwork. Challenge the class to identify the names of the different polygons used in the art. Ask students to describe their designs in their math journals.

SHAPE SORT

Objective

Students will compare and classify shapes according to size, color, and shape.

Anticipatory Set

Ahead of time, gather a set of attribute blocks for this activity. Prepare students for the activity by writing the following four lists on the board:

cat	*snake*	*shark*	*toucan*
dog	*lizard*	*halibut*	*canary*
lion	*alligator*	*tuna*	*parrot*
bear	*dinosaur*	*trout*	*blue jay*
skunk	*iguana*	*stingray*	*wren*

Ask students to name the group to which all of these items belong (*animals*). Then ask why you created four lists. What do the lists show? (*categories of animals*). Explain that the animal world is classified, or broken down, into groups according to certain features and characteristics. Ask students to identify each group (*mammals, reptiles, fish, birds*).

Explain that thousands of other items in the world can be classified into groups, such as cars, people, clothing, colors, food, and shapes.

> By offering problems that can be solved in different ways, we force students to spend more time analyzing the situation as they look for various solutions.

Purpose

Tell students that they will be classifying, or sorting, shapes into groups according to their features and characteristics.

Input

Place a handful of attribute blocks on each student's desk. Ask them to look carefully at the blocks. Ask, "What do you notice about these shapes? What do they have in common? How are they the same? How are they different?" Discuss students' responses. Place some on the overhead projector as well. Point out some similarities and differences among the shapes.

Modeling

Give students copies of the **Shape Sort reproducible (page 136).** Point out the three buckets. Explain that these buckets will help them sort and classify their shapes. Return to the overhead projector. Direct students to look at the different shapes displayed. Have them offer suggestions for different ways to classify the shapes. Suggestions might include size, shape, number of sides, number of angles, and so on. Follow a couple of the suggestions, sorting the shapes on the overhead projector. You might begin by labeling the first two buckets "Three Sides" and "Four Sides."

As you sort, explain your sorting rule: "I am sorting these according to sides. The shapes in this pile have three sides, and the shapes in this pile have four sides." Explain that when students sort their shapes, they will need to be able to explain their sorting rules. Trace some of the shapes in the appropriate buckets on the transparency.

Guided Practice

Erase your writing on the transparency. Next, explain that you will sort your shapes by number of sides and size. Invite students to follow along at their desks, sorting their shapes into separate groups. Label one bucket "Four Sides," one bucket "Small," and the last bucket "Four Sides and Small." Sort your shapes accordingly, pointing out that there are many attributes to use to sort the shapes.

Group students into pairs, and have them work together to decide how they will sort their shapes. Tell them to follow the directions on the reproducible.

Checking for Understanding

Ask students if they have any questions. Make sure students understand the task before letting them continue. Remind them that they may sort their shapes using two or three attributes, such as number of sides, color, and size.

Independent Practice

After they have sorted the shapes, give students copies of the **Shape Sort Questions reproducible (page 137)** to complete individually or with partners. They will use their answers to these questions in a class discussion.

Closure

Encourage students to share how they sorted their shapes. Then initiate a discussion based on students' answers on the Shape Sort Questions reproducible. Invite them to suggest all the ways the shapes could be sorted. Encourage students to record their classmates' suggestions in their math journals.

Shape Sort

Directions: Sort your shapes in the buckets. Label each bucket with your sorting rule. Then draw the shapes in the buckets where they belong.

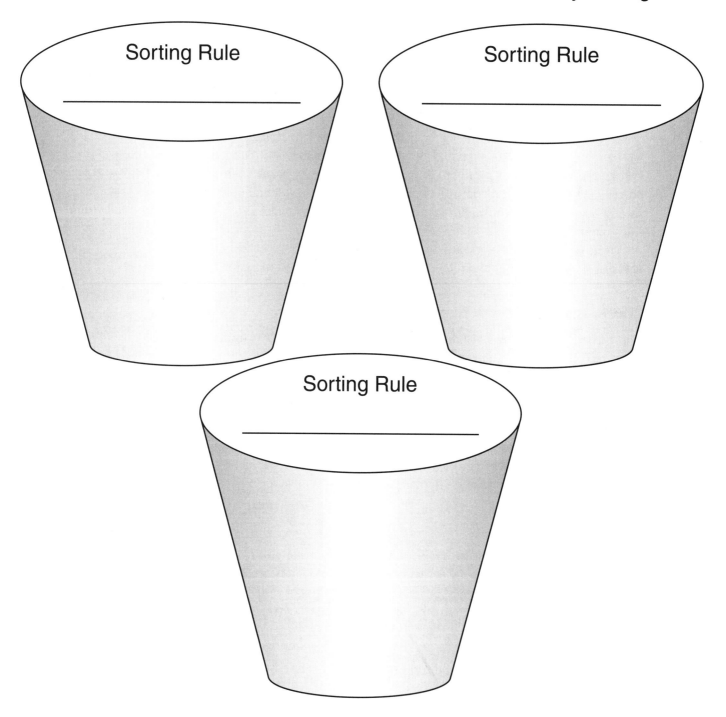

Sorting Rule
_____

Sorting Rule
_____

Sorting Rule
_____

Shape Sort Questions

Directions: Answer these questions about the Shape Sort activity.

1. How are the trapezoid and the parallelogram alike? How are they different?

_____

_____

_____

_____

2. What is another way you could have sorted your shapes?

_____

_____

_____

_____

3. What do all of the shapes have in common?

_____

_____

_____

4. Are there any shapes that don't fit with the others?

_____

_____

_____

_____

_____

7

Data Analysis

Let It Roll

Counting Candy

A Day at the Zoo

Button Bonanza

Weather Watchers

Picture Perfect

Hot and Cold

Eye-Catching Graphs

Survey Says

LET IT ROLL

Objectives

Students will make predictions based on probabilities.

Students will collect data and make a bar graph to present the data.

Anticipatory Set

Gather a collection of cubes in four colors—red, blue, green, and yellow. Ask students to help you count aloud as you place eight red cubes, six blue cubes, four green cubes, and two yellow cubes in a bag. Then ask students to identify which color cube is most likely to be drawn from the bag (*red*). Ask them to explain their reasoning (*There are more red cubes than any other color; therefore, red is most likely to be chosen.*). Shake the bag, and pass it around, allowing four students to draw one cube each from the bag. Make a tally mark on the board for each color cube drawn, and discuss the results.

Purpose

Tell students that they will predict which sum will appear most often when rolling a pair of dice. Then they will roll dice repeatedly, keep track of the sums of the numbers, and graph their results.

Input

Ask students to describe a tally mark. Discuss the purpose of making tally marks when collecting data. Explain that using tally marks is a quick and easy way of keeping track of numbers while counting data. Tell students that they will roll two dice and mark the sum of the roll on a chart using tally marks.

Modeling

Copy the **Let It Roll! Data Sheet** and **Let It Roll! Graph Sheet reproducibles (pages 142–143)** onto transparencies. Place the data sheet on the overheard projector. Point out the sentence frame at the top of the page, where students will write the sum they think will be rolled by two dice the most often. (Do not make a prediction at this point, as it may influence the students' predictions.) Ask a volunteer to provide a prediction for the sum, and write it on the reproducible.

Ask a student to roll a pair of dice and add the two numbers. Mark this sum with a tally mark on the data sheet. Pass the dice to five more students, and mark their sums on the data sheet as well. Then place the graph sheet on the overhead, and graph the results of your short demonstration.

Guided Practice

Give each student copies of the Let It Roll! Data Sheet and Let It Roll! Graph Sheet reproducibles and two dice. Tell them to take a moment to think about and record their predictions. Then ask them to roll the dice 20 times and record the sums. Walk around the room to make sure that students are adding numbers and recording sums correctly. After they have gathered their data, have students present their data on their graphs. Direct them to record at the bottom of the page which sum actually came up the most often and whether this confirmed their predictions.

Checking for Understanding

Draw a tally chart on the board, listing sums from 2 to 12. Ask each student to call out the sum that appeared most frequently. Record the students' answers on the chart. Engage students in a discussion about the sums that appeared most often. Ask questions such as, *Were you surprised by the results? Why or why not?* and *Do you understand why the sums that appeared most often were more likely to be rolled than other sums?*

Independent Practice

Invite students to craft their own probability experiments using different items. Provide colored chips, playing cards, coins, and other manipulatives for experimentation. Ask students to create collections that contain graduated numbers of different items. For example, if working with coins, students could use twice as many nickels as pennies and three times as many dimes as nickels. Encourage students to exchange their sets of items, make predictions about which items will be chosen most often, and then test their predictions. Make sure students record their data and then graph their results.

Closure

In their math journals, have students write about the experiments they created during Independent Practice. Ask them to draw pictures of the items they used and write about what they learned.

Let It Roll! Data Sheet

Directions: If you roll two dice, what sum do you think will appear most often? Write your prediction on the line. Then roll two dice 20 times. Use tally marks to record sums on the chart. Was your prediction correct?

My Prediction: I think the sum _____ will appear most often.

Sums	
2	
3	
4	
5	
6	
7	
8	
9	
10	
11	
12	

Name _____ Date _____

Let It Roll! Graph Sheet

Directions: Make a bar graph below. Use your data from the Let It Roll! Data Sheet.

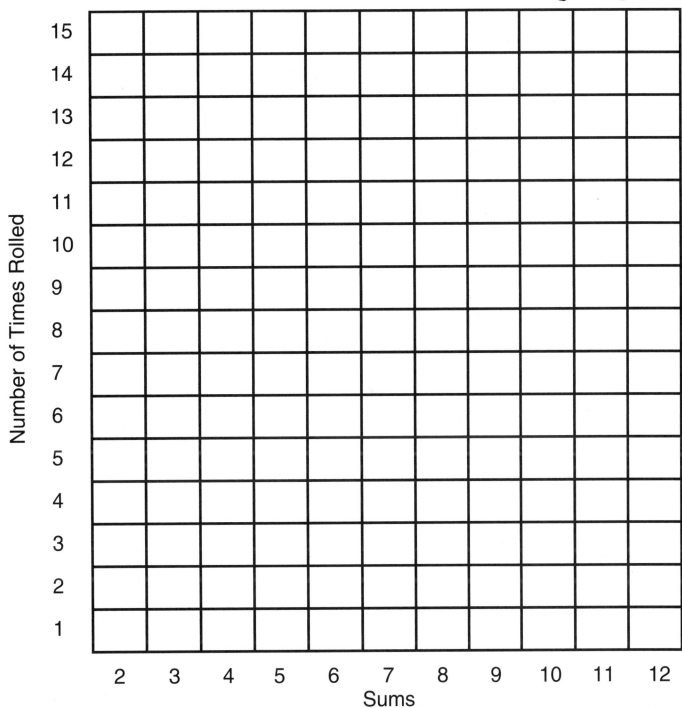

Number of Times Rolled (y-axis): 1, 2, 3, 4, 5, 6, 7, 8, 9, 10, 11, 12, 13, 14, 15

Sums (x-axis): 2, 3, 4, 5, 6, 7, 8, 9, 10, 11, 12

COUNTING CANDY

Objective

Students will collect, analyze, and graph data.

Anticipatory Set

Before beginning this activity, prepare a candy bag for each student. Place 1 cup of colored candies in each resealable plastic bag. Set aside the candy bags.

Survey your students about their favorite types of candy. Record their responses on the board using tally marks. For candies that come in different colors, such as jellybeans, ask which colors are students' favorites and make new tally charts to record those answers. Ask students to suggest ways that the information you collected could be organized.

Purpose

Tell students that they will each get a bag of candy to sort by color. After they sort the candies, they will use tally marks and a graph to record and present their results. Explain that they will work with two kinds of graphs—a bar graph and a pie chart.

Input

Explain that using graphs allows students to make easy comparisons between different objects or ideas. Demonstrate how to make a bar graph from the data collected earlier about students' favorite candy. After you have completed the graph, ask questions such as, *Which candy does the class like the most? Which candy does the class like the least?* and *How many more students prefer this candy to that one?*

Then demonstrate how to make a pie chart using the data collected earlier about students' favorite jellybean colors. Estimate aloud how to divide a circle into different-sized sections according to the data set. Draw a different pattern (or use a different color) for each section of the pie chart, and then make a corresponding pattern or color key.

Modeling

Open one bag of candy, and ask students to help you sort the candy by color. Invite a volunteer to write the color names in a column on the board. Then ask another volunteer to make tally marks by each color name for the candy colors you count. Draw a simple bar graph and pie chart on the board that represent the data. Invite students to help you transfer the data onto the charts. Then ask questions about the results, such as, *Which color in this bag appeared the most?* and *Which color appeared the least?*

Guided Practice

Give each student copies of the **Colorful Candy Data Sheet** and **Colorful Candy Graphs reproducibles (pages 146–147),** along with a bag of candy. Tell students to spread out the candies on their desks and sort them by color. Ask students to use the data sheet to tally the candy colors from their bags. Circulate around the room to make sure students are counting and recording numbers correctly.

When students have recorded their data, direct them to transfer those data to the graph sheet. On the bar graph, they should color one square for each candy color. On the pie chart, students should divide the circle into appropriate-sized sections for the candy colors. Note that some students may need assistance in deciding how to divide the pie chart. Assist as needed. Suggest that students color their graphs using colored pencils or crayons that correspond to the candy colors.

Checking for Understanding

Observe students as they complete the activity. Offer suggestions and guidance as needed to increase student understanding of data analysis.

Independent Practice

Encourage students to brainstorm survey questions to ask one another, such as, *What is your favorite TV show? How many siblings do you have? How do you get to school?* and *What is your favorite animal or pet?* Record sample questions on the board, and then invite each student to choose a different question. Provide time for students to interview each other and gather the data. Then instruct them to construct their own bar graphs or pie charts to show the results.

Closure

Have students turn to partners and take 2 minutes to discuss the activity. Then have them answer the following questions in their math journals: "Which type of graph do you think is best for showing data? Why do you think so?"

Colorful Candy Data Sheet

Directions: Sort your candy by color. Write the names of the colors in the chart below. Make tally marks on the chart to record the number of each color.

Color:	Color:
Color:	**Color:**
Color:	**Color:**

Name _____ Date _____

Colorful Candy Graphs

Directions: Make a bar graph and a pie chart to show your candy data. Use colors to match the candy colors.

Colors

Bar Graph for Candy Colors

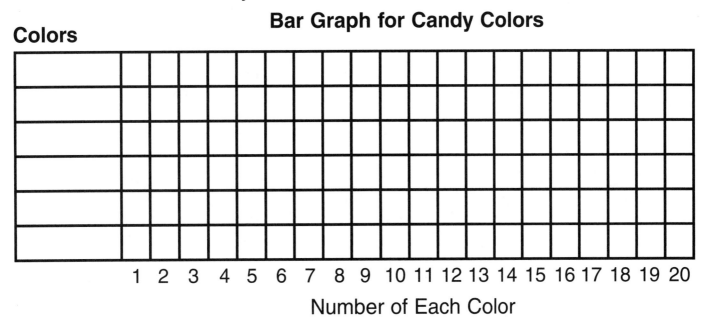

1 2 3 4 5 6 7 8 9 10 11 12 13 14 15 16 17 18 19 20

Number of Each Color

Graph Key

☐ _____

☐ _____

☐ _____

☐ _____

☐ _____

☐ _____

Pie Chart for Candy Colors

147

A DAY AT THE ZOO

Objectives

Students will read and interpret information from a story.

Students will graph information using one picture to represent two units.

Anticipatory Set

Display photographs of various zoo animals around your room. Ask students if they have ever been to a zoo, and encourage them to share their experiences.

> To help young students view numbers as values rather than labels, associate numbers with concrete objects.

Purpose

Tell students that they will read a rebus story about a day at the zoo. After reading the story, they will cut out pictures and create a graph of the animals mentioned in the story. Every picture used in the graph will represent two animals.

Input

Gather students into a line at the front of the classroom. Ask them how many shoes they are wearing all together. Review how to skip count by twos by counting the total number of shoes. Draw a stick-figure person on the board. Explain that the stick figure shows one student, but for your data set, it will represent two shoes. Have each student add a stick figure to the board next to yours. Then point to each figure as you count aloud by twos again.

Next, have students work in small groups to organize a variety of objects into pairs. For example, they can use crayons, pattern blocks, Unifix cubes, books, or markers. Have each group make a simple diagram to show how many items are in their collection. They should use one picture or symbol to represent every two items.

Modeling

Copy the **Zoo Day Rebus Story** and **Zoo Animal Cards reproducibles (pages 150–152)** onto transparencies. Cut out the animal cards, and set them aside. Have student volunteers take turns reading portions of the story aloud. After the story has been read once all the way through, go back and have students read sentences that describe the numbers of animals at the zoo. Pause after each sentence to discuss how the information could be depicted on a graph. For example, say, "This story tells us there are 16 monkeys at the zoo. I want to make a picture graph of the information. I will use one monkey picture to represent every 2 monkeys. How many monkey pictures do I need in my graph?" Ask a volunteer to use your picture cards to work out the problem on the overhead projector (*eight monkey pictures*).

Guided Practice

Tell students they will make their own graphs to show how many animals are at the zoo. Give them copies of the Zoo Day Rebus Story and Zoo Animal Cards reproducibles, highlighter pens, and large sheets of construction paper. Have students begin by highlighting information in the story that relates to the number of animals at the zoo. Then show them how to divide the construction paper into sections to make a grid for their graphs.

Remind students that each animal picture represents two animals. Choose one animal, and ask students to determine how many animal pictures should be on the graph, according to the story. Guide students through the process of attaching the appropriate number of animal pictures to the graph for the selected animal.

Checking for Understanding

Circulate around the room to monitor student work. Make sure that students have drawn and labeled eight columns with the animal names and have made at least 10 rows to represent up to 20 animals. Remind students to title their graphs and label the x- and y-axes. Assist as needed.

Independent Practice

Have students complete the rest of the graphs on their own. They should refer to the rebus story to gather the correct information for each animal.

Closure

Ask students to describe other graphs that can be made using one picture to represent two items. Have them brainstorm a list of possibilities. After brainstorming, have each student choose one graph idea from the list and write about it in his or her journal. Students can describe the pictures they would use and how they would collect the information they need to make the graph.

Zoo Day Rebus Story

Directions: Read the story. Then make a graph to show how many animals are at the zoo. Use one animal card for every two animals.

My family and I spent a day at the zoo. First we saw . All 4

of them were shooting water out of their trunks. Next, we saw the

. There were 16 of them in all. They chased each other

on the ropes and swings. Then we went to see the . 6 were busy

eating, but 2 of the small ones came right up to us! On our way to lunch,

we saw 6 . They had black and white and long necks.

After lunch, we visited the Reptile House. 10 slinky  were

wrapped around trees. Next door, there were 14  swimming

in a pond. We hiked up the road to see the . We saw 2 big brown

bears splashing in their pool. 2 more napped in their cave. At last

we reached Tiger Forest. A mother and her cub played with a big

. Our day was done. We had a roaring good time!

Zoo Animal Cards

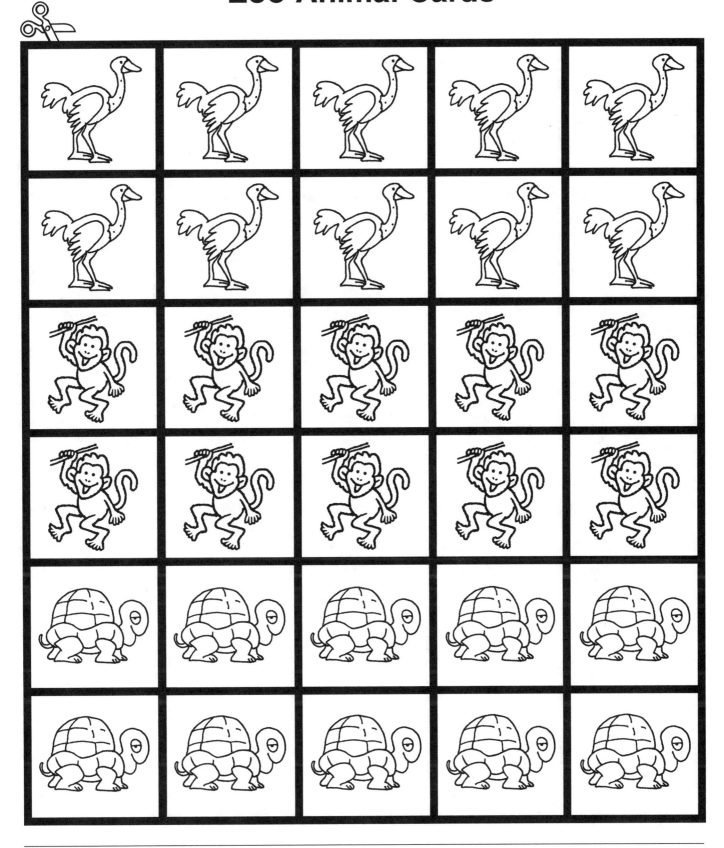

Zoo Animal Cards

BUTTON BONANZA

Objectives

Students will sort buttons by various attributes.

Students will use a Venn diagram to compare sets of buttons and record information in a chart.

Anticipatory Set

Ask students to examine any buttons they may have on their clothing. Encourage them to describe their buttons to the class. Then have them form groups based on the appearance of their buttons. Let students decide for themselves how to organize the groups. If they need help thinking of categories, suggest ideas such as color, size, shape, or number of buttonholes.

Purpose

Tell students that they will examine sets of buttons and think of ways to classify them. Then they will compare the buttons using a Venn diagram.

Input

Draw two interlocking circles on the board to make a Venn diagram. Point out how one side (or circle) of the diagram is used for one specific category or attribute and the other side is used for a different category or attribute. The section of the diagram where the two circles overlap represents attributes that both items share.

Label one side of your diagram "Has a Cat," and label the other side "Has a Dog." Then tell students, "If you have a cat but you do not have a dog, stand up." Write those students' names in the Has a Cat section of the diagram. Then say, "If you have a dog but you do not have a cat, stand up." Write those students' names in the Has a Dog section of the diagram. Finally, say, "If you have both a cat and a dog, stand up." Write those students' names in the overlapping section of the diagram. Point out how the circles cross over each other to include both attributes in that section.

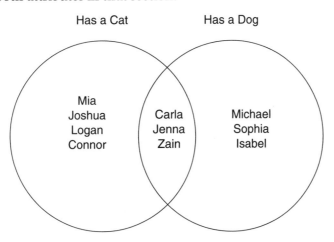

Encourage students to suggest other categories to diagram. Continue practicing as a group until you are confident that students understand how to use a Venn diagram.

Guided Practice

Divide the class into groups of four for this activity. Copy enough **Round Buttons, Square Buttons,** and **Heart Buttons reproducibles (pages 155–157)** onto heavy paper or cardstock so that each group has a set. Use different-colored paper for each reproducible. Then copy each reproducible onto a transparency to use for a demonstration.

Direct groups to cut out their button shapes. Then give each group two plastic hoops to lay on the floor in the shape of a Venn diagram. Call on one group to name an attribute, such as large buttons. Draw a Venn diagram on a transparency, and label one side "Large Buttons." Call on another group to name a different attribute, such as blue buttons. Label the other side of the diagram accordingly. Instruct students to work in their groups to organize all the large buttons and blue buttons in their Venn diagrams. Ask a volunteer to help you organize your buttons onto the transparency Venn diagram.

Use a transparency of the **Button Sort Record Sheet reproducible (page 158)** to show students how to record the results. Write "large buttons" for attribute A, "blue buttons" for attribute B, and "large, blue buttons" for attribute A + B. Then write the number of buttons for each attribute in the chart.

Checking for Understanding

Invite students to suggest two more attributes for sorting the buttons. Ask them to tell how they will demonstrate the attributes (organize the buttons) using a Venn diagram.

Independent Practice

Have students work in their groups to sort the buttons using three Venn diagrams. Remind them to record the attributes and numbers of buttons that match those attributes on their Button Sort Record Sheet.

Closure

Ask each group to present one of its Venn diagrams to the class. Allow students to use your overhead transparencies to demonstrate the attributes they used to sort the buttons. After the activity, have students draw a picture of one of their diagrams in their math journals. Encourage them to write one or two sentences describing how they sorted the buttons.

Round Buttons

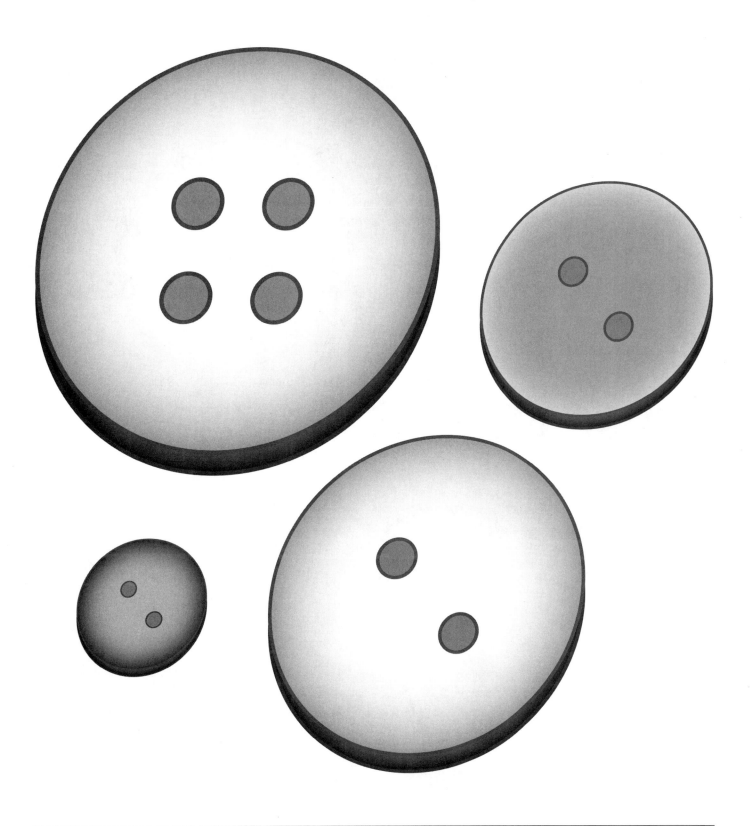

Square Buttons

Heart Buttons

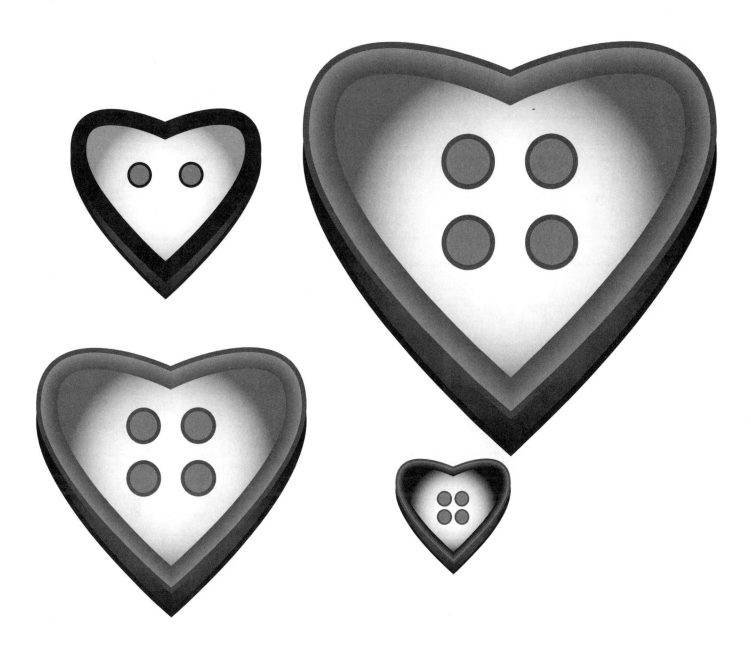

Button Sort Record Sheet

Directions: Work with your group to sort the buttons. Make three Venn diagrams to show how you sorted them. Write how you sorted the buttons. Then write the number of buttons that fit in each group.

	Attribute	Number of Buttons
A		
B		
A + B		

	Attribute	Number of Buttons
C		
D		
C + D		

	Attribute	Number of Buttons
E		
F		
E + F		

WEATHER WATCHERS

Objectives

Students will gather data about daily temperatures around the world.

Students will work in groups to organize data using graphs.

Anticipatory Set

Pack four suitcases with sets of adult-sized clothing for the different seasons. Include an equal number of items in each case. Here are some suggestions: winter—hat, earmuffs, sweater, coat, snow boots; spring—rain hat, scarf, long-sleeved T-shirt, rain coat, rain boots; summer—visor, sunglasses, T-shirt, shorts, sandals; fall—sweater, jacket, gloves, tennis shoes.

Tell students they will have a Weather Wardrobe relay race. Divide the class into four groups, and assign each one to a specific suitcase. Place the suitcases in a row several yards away from the groups. At your signal, have the first student in each line run to his or her suitcase and put on every item of clothing inside. The student then spins around three times in a circle, takes off the clothing items, puts the items back in the suitcase, and runs to the end of his or her group's line. The race continues until every player has had a turn taking part in the relay. The first group to get all of its players through the suitcases wins the race.

Purpose

Tell students that they will collect information about weather from different places around the world. They will use the information to create graphs that show daily temperatures in different locations.

> All students benefit when they use a variety of modalities while learning.

Input

Prior to beginning this activity, review a weather Web site to check for appropriate content. Show students how to access the selected Web site. Choose major cities from the six populated continents, and show students how to search for the daily high and low temperatures. Point out how the Web site uses icons to indicate certain weather conditions, such as a sun for sunny days or a rain cloud for rainy days.

Next, divide the class into six small groups. Assign each group to a continent, leaving out Antarctica. (You may want to explain that while Antarctica is a continent, there are no permanent residents or towns there.) Provide each group with a map of its continent, and direct students to choose one capital city shown on the map to study. Explain that a capital city is considered important in its region and is often where main government work is conducted. A capital city is usually marked with a star on a map.

Modeling

Choose a capital city that no other group has chosen, and use it as a model for the activity. Demonstrate how to use the weather Web site to look up the city's high and low temperatures for the day. Show students how to fill in the **Weather Watchers Data Sheet reproducible (page 161)** for today's temperatures. Record the names of the city, country, and continent on the sheet. Then write in the date on the chart, followed by the high and low temperatures. In the Weather Conditions box, draw a simple icon to indicate the weather conditions for the day.

Guided Practice

Help groups use the Web site to find the day's high and low temperatures for their selected cities. Guide them through the process of recording the information on the data sheet. Tell students that they will record the daily temperatures every day for a week. At the end of the week, they will use the data to make a graph for that city's daily temperatures.

Checking for Understanding

Ask each group to report its city's high and low temperature for the day and describe the weather conditions. Ask if it is a sunny day, a cloudy day, a rainy day, and so on. If students are able to relay the information accurately, then they are ready to proceed with the activity and collect data independently throughout the rest of the week.

Independent Practice

Provide groups with access to the computer each day so they can collect information for the Weather Watchers Data Sheet. At the end of the week, guide students in making graphs to show the data they collected. Allow groups to choose between bar graphs and line graphs. Demonstrate how to record two pieces of information for the same day. For example, if a group is making a bar graph, high temperatures might be indicated with red while low temperatures are indicated with blue. Have students draw weather icons on the graph to show what the weather conditions were like on each day.

Closure

Invite each group to present its graph to the class. Then have students respond to one of the following questions in their math journals: "How does knowing the temperature help people make decisions in their daily lives?" "What kinds of clothing do you think people in [name of city] wore this week?" or "What kinds of activities can people do there based on the weather?"

Weather Watchers Data Sheet

Directions: Find the daily temperature for your city. Write the date, the high temperature, and the low temperature every day for a week.

Group Members

The name of our city is _____

It is in the country of _____

It is on the continent of _____

Date	High Temperature	Low Temperature	Weather Conditions

PICTURE PERFECT

Objective

Students will create and analyze pictographs.

Anticipatory Set

Before beginning the activity, photocopy and cut out the cards on the **Topics Cards reproducible (page 164).** Put these topics cards in a bag or hat from which students can draw. Add more topics cards as desired. Set aside the cards.

To prepare students for the activity, draw the following symbols on the board: a bee and a happy face. Ask students what these symbols mean when put together (*Be happy.*). Then invite students to share other symbols they know and see every day on the street, in school, and around the community. Student responses might include a stop sign, a school crossing sign, a no smoking symbol, symbols to indicate the girls' and boys' bathrooms, a compass rose on a map, and so on. Ask students what each of these symbols means.

Purpose

Tell students that they will be using symbols to show a set of data.

Input

Explain that there is one type of graph in which symbols (or pictures) are used to represent the data. Ask if anyone knows what this type of graph is called (*pictograph*). Point out that *picto* in *pictograph* stands for *picture*. A pictograph is a graph that uses pictures to show data.

Modeling

Write "blue," "green," "red," and "other" on the board. Ask students to raise their hands if their favorite color is blue. Count and record the number on the board next to the word *blue*. Ask students to raise their hands if their favorite color is green. Count and record the number on the board next to the word *green*. Continue with the color *red* and *other*, recording data for each count.

Explain that you just conducted a survey. When someone conducts a survey, he or she gathers data and shows results in a logical, organized way. Display for students samples of various types of graphs, such as circle (pie) graphs, bar graphs, line graphs, and pictographs. Tell students that they will use pictographs in this activity.

To make a pictograph, students need to decide on a picture or symbol to represent their data. Display a transparency of the **Picture Perfect Pictograph reproducible (page 165)** on the overhead projector. Hold up a crayon and say, "Since this is a graph about favorite colors, I am going to use a crayon as my symbol." Draw a crayon in the Graph Key. Explain that the key shows what each picture represents. Explain that each crayon represents two students, so you are writing "2 students" on the line after the symbol in the key.

Label each row of your graph with one of the colors, and draw symbols to represent your data. Explain that each graph must have a title to show what kind of data the graph displays. Write a title for your graph, such as "Favorite Colors."

Checking for Understanding

Check to make sure students understand how to create a pictograph on their reproducibles. Encourage them to use simple symbols that are easy to show on their graph, such as circles, stars, or hearts. Encourage them to look around the classroom for ideas, or distribute small stickers from which students can choose.

Independent Practice

Have each student select a topic from the bag. Then invite students to survey their classmates about that topic. Give students plenty of time to make sure they get to survey everyone in the class. Once they have collected their data, have students go back to their seats to complete their pictographs.

Closure

Invite students to share their pictographs in small groups. Then have them write a response in their math journals to the following question: "What are the advantages of using a pictograph?"

Topics Cards

Favorite Pet	Favorite Breakfast Food	Favorite Kind of Sandwich
Favorite Flavor of Ice Cream	Favorite School Subject	Favorite Sport
Favorite Book Genre	Favorite Drink	Favorite Board Game
Favorite Hobby	Favorite Season	Eye Color
Hair Color	Number of Siblings	Favorite Kind of Shoes
Favorite Sports Team	Favorite Car	Favorite Ocean Animal
Favorite TV Show	Favorite Fast Food Restaurant	Favorite Kind of Music

Name _____   Date _____

Picture Perfect Pictograph

Directions: Show your data using the pictograph below.

Title: _____

Graph Key
☐ = _____

Number of Students

HOT AND COLD

Objective

Students will create and analyze line graphs.

Anticipatory Set

For at least a week before this activity, record the high and low temperatures for several cities. You may do this yourself or set a classroom computer to The Weather Channel Web site at www.weather.com. Assign a major city to each student. Allow students to take turns going to the computer and recording the high and low temperatures for their assigned cities using the **Temperature Record reproducible (page 168).** Make sure to assign yourself a city as well and keep track of those temperatures.

Engage students' attention by putting on clothes that are the opposite of those normally worn for the current weather in your area, such as a raincoat and boots (and carry an umbrella) if it is sunny outside or board shorts, a T-shirt, and sunglasses if it is snowing outside. Tell students, "I don't know how this happened! How was I supposed to know it would be [hot/cold] out today?" Students will probably tell you that you should have checked a weather report. Act surprised, and then ask why you should check the weather report. Students should explain that a weather report can tell you how hot or cold the temperature will be so you can dress appropriately.

> One way to help learners find meaning is to connect what they are learning to their daily lives.

Purpose

Tell students that they will be using a week's worth of temperature data to make a line graph of the high and low temperatures in a major city.

Input

Ask students what they know about line graphs. Explain that a line graph uses points connected by a line. Each point records a piece of data, and the overall line shows a series of data. This type of graph helps them to observe changes in a set of data over time. Show students several examples of simple line graphs. Point out how the line falls and rises, providing information that can cover an extended time.

Modeling

Place a transparency of the Temperature Record reproducible on the overhead projector, and display the data collected about your city. Point out that you have recorded high and low temperatures for the past week. You will use this information to create your line graph. Both sets of data—high temperatures and low temperatures—will be displayed on the same graph using different colors. Students will use one color to plot the high temperatures for the week and a different color to plot the low temperatures for the week.

Replace the Temperature Record transparency with a transparency of the **Graph reproducible (page 169).** Distribute photocopies of the reproducible to students. Tell students that they will label their graphs before they begin plotting any data. Write a title on the top of your graph, and invite students to title their own graphs with their assigned cities. Then show students how you number the left side of the graph in 10-degree increments. On the diagonal lines at the bottom of the graph, show students how you write the dates for your data set. Invite students to follow along on their reproducibles.

Using a red overhead marker, plot the points for the high temperatures for each day in your data set. When you have plotted all seven points, connect the line.

Guided Practice

For the low temperature data, call on volunteers to help you plot each point and draw the line on the overhead using a blue marker. Explain that students will plot high and low temperatures for their own cities on their reproducibles.

Checking for Understanding

While you are watching students complete this guided activity, offer any suggestions that may facilitate understanding. Make sure they understand how to proceed before allowing them to work independently.

Independent Practice

Have each student use his or her own city's data to complete a graph displaying the high and low temperatures for the week. Remind them to use different colors for the high and low temperatures.

Closure

Have students meet in small groups to discuss the differences between the temperatures of their cities. Then extend the activity by inviting each group to create a new line graph. For this graph, they will plot each city's average high or low temperature so they can see a visual comparison between the cities' average temperatures across the week.

Afterward, ask students to reflect on the activity in their math journals. Encourage them to list several more data sets for which a line graph would be appropriate.

Name _____ **Date** _____

Temperature Record for _____

Directions: Write the name of your city on the line. Record the high and low temperatures for that city every day for a week.

Day/Date	High Temperature	Low Temperature

Graph for

Directions: Use the data you collected about your city to make a line graph. Make sure to label the different parts of the graph.

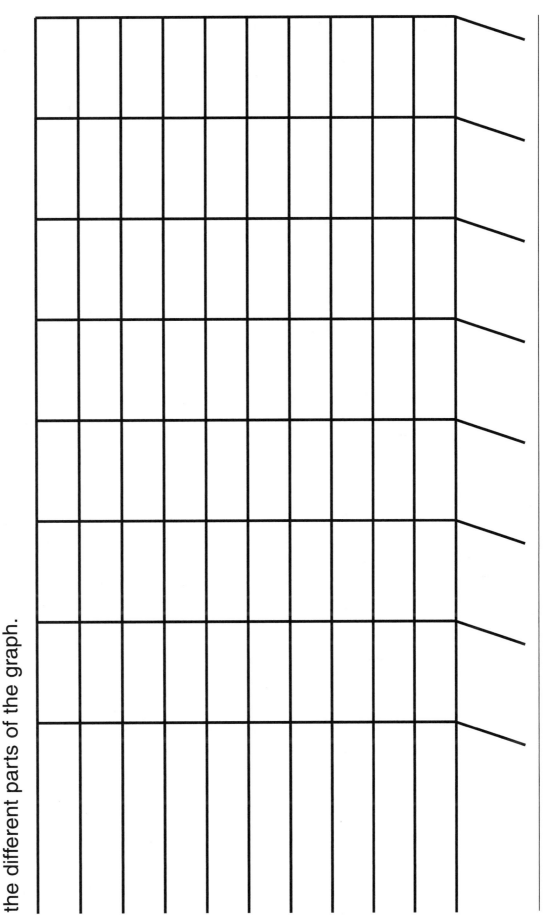

EYE-CATCHING GRAPHS

Objective

Students will create and analyze circle graphs.

Anticipatory Set

Make sure colored pencils are available for this activity. Walk around the room, peering into the eyes of several students. Ask them to tell you the color of their eyes. After walking around the classroom, list all the eye colors you observed, such as blue, brown, hazel, and green.

Purpose

Tell students that they are going to use their eye colors as part of a data set to practice making circle graphs.

Input

Explain that circle graphs, sometimes called pie graphs, help display the parts of a whole. Each section represents a part of the complete data set. This type of graph makes using fractions or decimals easy when discussing or showing data.

Modeling

Write "green," "blue," "brown," and "hazel" on the board. Explain that you surveyed six teachers to find out their eye color, and two had green eyes. Make two tally marks underneath *green*. Continue, explaining that two teachers had blue eyes, one had brown eyes, and one had hazel eyes. Make the corresponding tally marks on the board.

Explain that your whole data set consists of six teachers. The graph you complete will have six sections, each representing one part of the whole set. Place a transparency of the **Eye-Catching Circle Graph reproducible (page 172)** on the overhead. Count the sections of the blank circle graph with students. Tell them that you will be coloring one section for each teacher. Ask students how many teachers had green eyes. Color in two adjacent sections of the circle graph with a green marker. Explain to students that the sections should be next to each other so when the graph is finished, you can tell at a glance which colors occurred more or less often. These two smaller sections make up one bigger section, or piece, of data.

Guided Practice

Have volunteers come to the overhead and color the correct number of sections for each of the other colors. When the graph is complete, have students interpret the data. Ask questions: "Which fraction of the teachers had green eyes?" (²/₆ *or* ¹/₃), "Which fraction of the teachers had hazel eyes?" (¹/₆), and "How many more teachers had blue eyes than brown eyes?" (*one*).

Independent Practice

Divide the class into mixed-ability groups of six. Give each group a copy of the Eye-Catching Circle Graph reproducible. Group members will work together to create a circle graph for a set of data. Have each student color in a section of the circle graph that corresponds with his or her eye color. Tell students to use colored pencils that match their eye colors and color matching sections next to each other.

Closure

Gather the class back together into a large group. Work with students to compile the individual group data into a large class circle graph to display on a bulletin board. Challenge students to label each section of the graph with fractions and percentages. Discuss your results.

Ask students to work with partners to think of other data sets for which a circle graph would be appropriate. Have them write their ideas in their math journals.

Eye-Catching Circle Graph

Directions: Use this circle graph to graph data about eye color in your group.

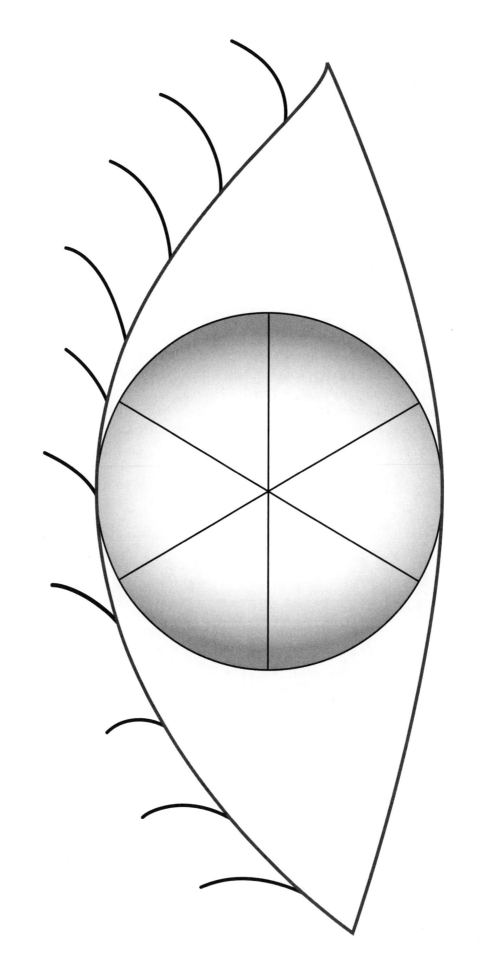

SURVEY SAYS

Objective

Students will collect data and use different methods to represent data in various graphs.

Anticipatory Set

Ask students if they have ever seen the popular television game show *Family Feud*. In this game, families compete to think of the most popular answers to common, everyday questions. Each answer is ranked according to how many people in a survey answered in a particular way. Demonstrate the meaning of *survey* by asking students to name their favorite food. Write students' responses on the board as in the following example.

Hamburgers	*11*
Pizza	*7*
Chicken	*2*
Hot dogs	*3*
Spaghetti	*1*
Tacos	*5*

Point out that in this survey, the most popular answer is *hamburgers* because it received the most votes. The second most popular answer is *pizza*, followed by *tacos* and *hot dogs*. Explain that the results of this survey can be used to play a variation of the game show called Survey Says!

Purpose

Tell students that they will conduct their own surveys and decide which type of graph would best display the data set collected. They will use their completed graphs to play a class game of Survey Says!

> Ask students to examine data using graphs, formulas, and other comparisons.

Input

Reinforce learning by asking students to describe the meaning of *survey* and how a survey is conducted. Discuss the idea that a survey is a way of gathering and collecting information or opinions about different topics to create a database. These data can then be displayed in an easy-to-read format, such as a bar graph, line graph, circle graph, or pictograph.

Modeling

Use the information from your survey in the Anticipatory Set to create a simple circle or bar graph on the board. Invite students to help you create the graph and record the data. Tell students that they will work in groups to survey their classmates. As a class, brainstorm common, everyday topics students could use to survey classmates. Write each topic on a separate index card; examples of topics are best place to study, easiest school subject, hardest school subject, favorite TV show, best cafeteria lunch, and favorite summer activity.

Divide the class into small survey groups. You might create groupings based on mixed abilities or interest. Then assign each group or invite each group to choose one topic for a class survey. Or you can write topics on index cards and have students draw cards from a bag or box.

Guided Practice

Distribute construction paper, scissors, glue, and crayons or markers for students to use to create their graphs. Help students as they conduct their surveys and create graphs. Students should choose the graphs that they believe best displays their data. You might also choose to assign a different type of graph to each group. If you wish, include other classes in the surveys.

Checking for Understanding

Before students begin their surveys, make sure they understand how to collect data accurately (such as using tally marks) and how to create each type of graph. Help them select the most appropriate graphs to display their data. Make sure they check with you before making final selections.

Independent Practice

Have students complete their graphs. As they are working, circulate around the room, and provide assistance as needed. Make sure each graph clearly shows the range of survey results, from most popular answers to least popular answers.

Closure

Close this graphing activity by playing an exciting class game of Survey Says! Tell students that their partners or groups will now become teams that complete against each other to guess the most popular answers from the surveys to gain points.

Collect all the graphs. Invite two teams to begin the game. Call out a survey question, such as, "What do your classmates say is their favorite cafeteria lunch?" The first player to "buzz in" with a bell or a raised hand gets a chance to answer the question. After the player makes a guess, reveal the most popular answer by dramatically calling out, "Survey says . . ." and then giving the answer.

If the player's answer is the most popular, according to the graph, he or she receives the corresponding number of points for his or her team. For example, if the survey states that 10 students chose hamburgers as their favorite cafeteria lunch, the player's team receives 10 points.

The team that guesses the most popular answer then gets to continue guessing the rest of the most popular lunches until they miss two. Then it's the next team's turn to guess. Continue playing the game until all graphs are used and all teams have had a chance to play. The team with the most points accumulated wins.

After the game, ask students to reflect on their learning in their math journals. Ask them to write about how making graphs helps to show different kinds of data. Prompt them with questions such as, *Which kind of graph do you think is easiest to make? Which kind of graph do you think is easiest to read?* and *Which kind of graph do you think shows data the most clearly?*

Name _____ **Date** _____

Journal Page

1. What did I learn today?

_____

_____

_____

_____

2. How does what I learned add to something I already know?

_____

_____

_____

_____

3. How can what I learned help me later on?

_____

_____

_____

_____

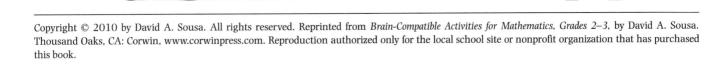

Answer Key

Order Up! (page 10)

1. 17, 65, 103, 212, 920
2. 4, 62, 462, 463, 1,000
3. 1, 15, 108, 653, 831
4. 318, 394, 444, 768, 823
5. 7, 10, 79, 85, 100

Stretching Numbers (page 17)

1. $300 + 70 + 3$
2. $1,000 + 200 + 30 + 1$
3. $400 + 20 + 2$
4. $3,000 + 700 + 80 + 9$
5. $8,000 + 600 + 70 + 1$

Toss It! Practice (page 30)

1. 11
2. 57
3. 35
4. 52
5. 53
6. 63
7. 75
8. 65
9. 59
10. 49

Math Hockey Practice (page 34)

1. 110
2. 70
3. 50
4. 220
5. 120
6. 130
7. 110

8. 80
9. 110
10. 30

Tray Arrays (page 43)

1. $3 \times 7 = 21$
2. $2 \times 8 = 16$
3. $5 \times 6 = 30$
4. $4 \times 4 = 16$

Grape Groups (page 47)

1. $18 \div 3 = 6$
2. $20 \div 4 = 5$
3. $12 \div 2 = 6$
4. $25 \div 5 = 5$

Button Fact Families (page 50)

1. Fact Family: 2, 6, 12

   $6 \times 2 = 12$
   $2 \times 6 = 12$
   $12 \div 6 = 2$
   $12 \div 2 = 6$

2. Fact Family: 3, 8, 24

   $3 \times 8 = 24$
   $8 \times 3 = 24$
   $24 \div 3 = 8$
   $24 \div 8 = 3$

3. Fact Family: 4, 7, 28

   $4 \times 7 = 28$
   $7 \times 4 = 28$
   $28 \div 7 = 4$
   $28 \div 4 = 7$

4. Fact Family: 2, 9, 18

   $2 \times 9 = 18$
   $9 \times 2 = 18$
   $18 \div 2 = 9$
   $18 \div 9 = 2$

5. Fact Family: 6, 7, 42

$6 \times 7 = 42$

$7 \times 6 = 42$

$42 \div 7 = 6$

$42 \div 6 = 7$

8. Fact Family: 10, 4, 40

$4 \times 10 = 40$

$10 \times 4 = 40$

$40 \div 4 = 10$

$40 \div 10 = 4$

Opposites Attract (page 53)

1. $12 \times 2 = 24$

$24 \div 12 = 2$ or $24 \div 2 = 12$

2. $5 \times 6 = 30$

$30 \div 5 = 6$ or $30 \div 6 = 5$

3. $11 \times 8 = 88$

$88 \div 11 = 8$ or $88 \div 8 = 11$

4. $9 \times 3 = 27$

$27 \div 9 = 3$ or $27 \div 3 = 9$

5. $8 \times 4 = 32$

$32 \div 8 = 4$ or $32 \div 4 = 8$

6. $7 \times 10 = 70$

$70 \div 7 = 10$ or $70 \div 10 = 7$

7. $12 \times 8 = 96$

$96 \div 12 = 8$ or $96 \div 8 = 12$

8. $7 \times 6 = 42$

$42 \div 7 = 6$ or $42 \div 6 = 7$

9. $5 \times 11 = 55$

$55 \div 5 = 11$ or $55 \div 11 = 5$

10. $10 \times 3 = 30$

$30 \div 10 = 3$ or $30 \div 3 = 10$

Draw and Divide (page 59)

1. $32 \div 8 = 4$
2. $40 \div 5 = 8$
3. $49 \div 7 = 7$
4. $27 \div 9 = 3$
5. $12 \div 4 = 3$

6. $16 \div 2 = 8$
7. $54 \div 9 = 6$
8. $22 \div 2 = 11$

Fruity Fractions (page 64)

1. $\frac{1}{9}, \frac{1}{8}, \frac{1}{4}$
2. $\frac{2}{9}, \frac{2}{5}, \frac{2}{3}$
3. $\frac{9}{32}, \frac{9}{23}, \frac{9}{12}$
4. $\frac{5}{8}, \frac{5}{7}, \frac{5}{6}$
5. $\frac{4}{15}, \frac{4}{9}, \frac{4}{6}$
6. $\frac{3}{47}, \frac{3}{15}, \frac{3}{8}$
7. $\frac{1}{85}, \frac{1}{79}, \frac{1}{74}$
8. $\frac{8}{13}, \frac{8}{12}, \frac{8}{9}$
9. $\frac{6}{60}, \frac{6}{50}, \frac{6}{30}$
10. $\frac{4}{8}, \frac{4}{7}, \frac{4}{6}$

Treasure Hunt Clues (page 72)

You can find your hidden treasure where the teacher sits.

Take a Bigger Bite! Activity 1 (page 75)

1. <
2. >
3. >
4. <
5. >
6. >
7. >
8. >
9. <
10. >
11. <
12. >
13. <
14. >
15. <
16. <

**Take a Bigger Bite! Activity 2
(page 76)**

1. <
2. >
3. =
4. <
5. =
6. <
7. >
8. <
9. >
10. <
11. <
12. >

Fraction Cookie Bars (page 79)

Doubled Recipe:

2 cups softened butter

4 cups sugar

8 eggs

4 tsp. vanilla

$2\frac{2}{3}$ cups flour

$1\frac{1}{2}$ cups unsweetened cocoa

2 tsp. baking powder

1 tsp. salt

$1\frac{1}{3}$ cups chopped nuts

$\frac{2}{3}$ cup butter

12 ounces softened cream cheese

$\frac{2}{3}$ cup sugar

4 Tbs. flour

4 eggs

$1\frac{1}{2}$ tsp. vanilla

**Carpeting the Classrooms
(page 106)**

My classroom measurements will vary.

Miss Chang's classroom: P = 140 ft;
A = 1,125 sq ft; Carpeting = $2,812.50

Miss Griffith's classroom: P = 142 ft;
A = 1,248 sq ft; Carpeting = $3,120.00

Mrs. Garcia's classroom: P = 134 ft;
A = 1,080 sq ft; Carpeting = $2,700.00

Mr. Green's classroom: P = 138 ft;
A = 1,190 sq ft; Carpeting = $2,975.00

Mrs. Owen's classroom: P = 142 ft;
A = 1,104 sq ft; Carpeting = $2,760.00

Final square footage will vary, depending on "My Classroom" measurements.

Final carpeting cost will vary, depending on "My Classroom" measurements.

**Shape-y Shake-y Practice
(page 121)**

1. cylinder
2. cube
3. pyramid
4. cone
5. sphere
6. rectangular prism

**Letter Symmetry Record Sheet
(page 128)**

A Day at the Zoo (page 150)

Student graphs should show the following numbers of animal cards: 2 elephants, 8 monkeys, 4 giraffes, 10 ostriches, 5 snakes, 7 turtles, 2 bears, and 1 tiger.

References

A to Z Teacher Stuff. (1997–2006). *Graphing*. Retrieved December 20, 2007, from http://www.atozteacherstuff.com/Lesson_Plans/Mathematics/__Grades_K–2/Graphing/index.shtml

Annenberg Media Learner.org. (1997–2008). *Interactives: Geometry 3D shapes*. Retrieved December 20, 2007, from http://www.learner.org/interactives/geometry/

Encyclopaedia Britannica Online. (2008). *Learning theory*. Retrieved December 12, 2007, from http://www.britannica.com/eb/article-9108413/learning-theory

Jensen, E. P. (2005). *Brain-based learning: The new science of teaching and training*. Thousand Oaks, CA: Corwin.

Lanius, C. (1998–2007). *Pattern blocks*. Retrieved December 20, 2007, from http://math.rice.edu/~lanius/images/4_polygo.gif

Mankus, M. L. (1998). *Pattern block grid*. Retrieved December 20, 2007, from http://mason.gmu.edu/~mmankus/PBlocks/pbgrid.htm

National Council of Teachers of Mathematics. (2005). *Principles and standards for school mathematics*. Reston, VA: Author.

National Council of Teachers of Mathematics. (2008). *Curriculum focal points for prekindergarten through grade 8 mathematics: Grade 2*. Retrieved December 18, 2007, from http://www.nctm.org/standards/focalpoints.aspx?id=330&ekmensel=c580fa7b_10_52_330_5

Perry, B. D. (n.d.). *How the brain learns best*. Retrieved December 1, 2007, from http://teacher.scholastic.com/professional/bruceperry/brainlearns.htm

PLOS Biology, Public Library of Science. (2005, June 7). *Cutting through the clutter: How the brain learns to see*. Retrieved December 5, 2007, from http://biology.plosjournals.org/perlserv/?request=get-document&doi=10.1371/journal.pbio.0030256&ct=1

Sousa, D. A. (2006). *How the brain learns* (3rd ed.). Thousand Oaks, CA: Corwin.

Sousa, D. A. (2008). *How the brain learns mathematics*. Thousand Oaks, CA: Corwin.

Tate, M. L. (2003). *Worksheets don't grow dendrites: 20 instructional strategies that engage the brain*. Thousand Oaks, CA: Corwin.